A practical guide to
Cage and Aviary Birds

An oasis hummingbird, displaying its brilliantly sequined throat.

A male zebra finch, named for the striped markings on its breast.

A practical guide to Cage and Aviary Birds

Rob Harvey

Photographs by Cyril Laubscher

TIGER BOOKS INTERNATIONAL
LONDON

3291
This edition published in 1994 by Tiger Books International PLC, London
© 1994 Coombe Books
Printed and Bound in Singapore
All rights reserved.
ISBN 1-85501-416-5

Credits
Edited and designed: Ideas into Print
Typesetting: Ideas into Print and Ash Setting and Printing
Production Director: Gerald Hughes
Production: Ruth Arthur, Sally Connolly, Neil Randles

THE AUTHOR

Rob Harvey is the director and curator of Birdworld, founded in 1968 by his father, Roy Harvey, and now the largest collection of birds in the UK. In 1988 Rob designed and built the incubation research station, which is renowned worldwide for its discoveries. Since publishing his first book entitled 'Practical Incubation', he has travelled around the world as an avicultural consultant, advising on all aspects of the subject, from designing bird parks to training staff.

THE PHOTOGRAPHER

Cyril Laubscher has travelled extensively in Europe, Australia, Southern Africa and South America photographing wildlife. To augment his photography in the wild, he has developed special techniques for photographing birds and animals in studio conditions. His work has been featured in photographic exhibitions, and in numerous books and journals.

THE CONSULTANT

Allan Brooker began keeping birds in 1960. His first birds were zebra finches, but since then he has kept most types of birds except birds of prey. Some of his birds are pictured in this book. His main interest is breeding birds and he has several first breedings to his credit. He participates in competitive bird shows and is a member of the Avicultural Society.

A pearl cockatiel, one of many colour varieties of these popular pet birds.

CONTENTS

A masked lovebird, clearly showing its black face, or 'mask'.

Two canary-winged parakeets show off their acrobatic skills. These South American birds can become tame and hardy.

AN INTRODUCTION TO KEEPING BIRDS

For whatever reason you wish to keep birds, whether as a pet, for display or because you are interested in breeding, never rush into buying them. Visit several pet stores and bird farms first to determine what type of bird you wish to keep and whether it is practical for you to keep it.

If you are looking for a pet bird, be sure to choose a bird that is already tame. But be careful, even the tamest of birds can turn wild for various reasons. If you wish to keep a collection of birds in an outside aviary and this seems perfectly possible during the summer months, check that the birds you choose can cope with a typical winter in your area. Some birds need to be locked into a shelter - perhaps with heat and lighting - at night. Do you have facilities for this?

If you are considering breeding your birds, remember that you will need specialized equipment and materials, such as nestboxes and extra food for the new chicks. Also, take into account that while they are breeding, your birds will need more privacy than those kept purely for display, and if you are successful, you will need spare enclosures in which to keep the newly weaned youngsters.

It is extremely important to buy healthy birds from the outset. If you have very little experience of keeping birds, you may not know what an ill bird looks like. This is why it is a good idea to visit various bird collections, for you will soon appreciate which birds are healthy and which are not.

When you go to buy your birds, take an experienced birdkeeper with you. If you do not know such a person, make contact with your local bird club or with a bird magazine that might have details of local breeders who could show you their collections and advise you in general.

Introducing and handling birds

Below: This very strong carrying cage would mainly be used for transporting parrots that are slightly tame. If the bird is nervous, cover the cage with a towel.

Below: These cardboard carrying boxes are provided by pet shops for most birds except parrots. They keep the birds in the dark, which is less stressful for them. Notice the large number of air holes.

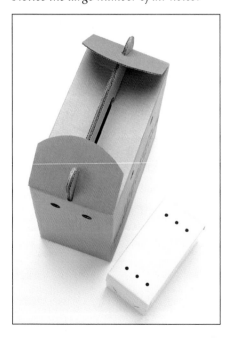

Before buying your first pet bird or adding a new one to an established collection, you must ask some important questions and use the answers to decide how to acclimatize your birds with minimum stress.

Keeping stress to a minimum

First find out what conditions the bird has been kept in for the previous few months. Has the bird been kept inside or outside? If it has been housed inside, establish the temperature at which it has been kept. If it has been kept outside, find out whether the aviary was completely out in the open or whether it was well sheltered. Also ask whether it has been kept with other birds; it can be quite a shock for a bird to be suddenly introduced into a colony when it has been used to being by itself.

An important question to ask is how the bird has been fed. When you have discovered what the bird has been used to eating, try to feed it the same diet for the first couple of weeks, even if you do not approve of the diet. Then you can slowly introduce it to the foods you feel are more suitable. If you immediately feed the bird a completely different diet, this abrupt change - in conjunction with its move to unfamiliar surroundings - will raise the bird's stress level considerably. Since it is highly disturbing for a bird to be moved from one place to another, these simple precautions will help to keep the stress level low.

Another way of lowering stress is to provide the bird with a little extra heat during its first few days. This is easy to do indoors simply by increasing the temperature of the room. You can raise the temperature in an outdoor, sheltered aviary by turning on an infrared lamp for a few days.

If you plan to keep your new bird in a cage in your home, it is a good idea to place an old towel over the cage for the first day. This not only provides warmth, but also a sense of security for the bird while it familiarizes itself with its new enclosure. If your new bird is destined to live in an outside aviary, do not suddenly release it into the aviary. It is likely that the bird will fly into the wire and injure itself. It is also advisable to cover any glass or clear plastic panels in the aviary with paper or whitewash so that they are no longer transparent. This will prevent distressed and confused birds from colliding with the panels. A good strategy is to leave the new bird in a small wire cage inside the aviary for a day so that it can become used to its new surroundings. Then you can open the door of the cage and let the bird come out in its own time; do not force it to come

Right: When it comes to holding birds, the basic rule is to be gentle but firm and be careful of the windpipe. It is a good idea to use gloves when handling larger birds, as they can bite. The problem with wearing gloves, however, is that it is more difficult to know where or what you are touching and how much pressure you are exerting. Even through gloves, a parrot is still capable of giving you a severe bite. You may believe that your tame bird will not bite you when you try to catch it to clip its nails or wings. Do not be deceived; tame birds can and will bite when caught.

Below: This shows how to hold a small bird, such as a budgerigar, gently but firmly using one hand. Hardly any pressure is put on the throat of the bird.

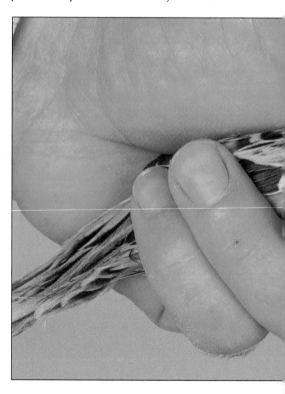

out. Once the bird is familiar with its surroundings, you can clean off or remove the coverings from any transparent panels.

Always give new birds several food and water dishes around the aviary. Do not be alarmed if your bird does not immediately hunt for food; this is quite normal. After a few days, your bird will know where all the food and water dishes are and you can then slowly remove them until only one food and one water dish remain.

Although it may not eat for the first few hours or so, once it becomes familiar with its surroundings check that your bird is eating properly. Just because the food dish is being emptied, this does not necessarily mean that the bird is eating - it could just be pecking through its food trying to find something it likes. One way to confirm that your bird is eating is to check for droppings. Supplements containing vitamins and trace elements are available that you can add to your birds' food during the first few days. These can help to sustain the bird when its digestive system is not working properly because of increased stress levels.

Try to avoid any disturbance during the first few days by introducing it to one new thing at a time. If you have any pets, acquaint them very gradually. A common problem is with cats. You may not keep a cat yourself, but any local cats will soon become aware of a new bird in the neighbourhood. Do not think that your bird is perfectly safe just because the cat cannot get to it; the sudden appearance of a cat can literally scare a bird to death.

If your bird has been kept in an indoor environment, such as quarantine, and you eventually plan to house it outside, keep it inside for a period and provide a shallow water bowl in the cage in which it can bathe. A dish with angled rather than straight sides is best and perhaps with a few stones at the bottom to help the bird get out. This approach will also help to acquaint the bird with rain. If you put the bird outside and there is a downpour of rain, it can become waterlogged and then extremely cold.

Transferring birds safely

Before transferring your bird from the carrying box to the cage, there are a few simple rules to follow. In an indoor environment, make sure that all the windows and doors are shut before you take the bird out of the box and into the cage. If the bird is to be kept in an outdoor aviary, carry the box containing the bird into the aviary and then release it. Whatever you do, do not take the bird out of the box by hand and then walk over to the aviary to release it. (In any case, as advised earlier, it is a good idea to keep a new bird in a cage within the aviary for the first few days.) To make the task of removing a bird from a small cage a little easier, be sure to remove all the perches in the cage. Otherwise, you may spend a couple of minutes chasing the bird around the cage with your hand.

Contact a veterinarian

If you are not in touch with a local veterinarian, it is a good idea to make contact before you acquire any birds. This is because if your bird suddenly becomes ill, the sooner you can get expert help, the better.

Using a net

If you have to catch a bird from an aviary you will need a good net. This should be large enough to enable you to catch the bird easily, and since you will need to move the net quickly and swiftly, it must have a padded rim to prevent damaging the bird. (See the one shown on page 24.) Ensure that the net is deep enough so that once the bird is inside, you can turn the handle so that the net folds over and traps the bird securely. Avoid chasing a bird around an aviary for a long time. If the weather is hot and one person with a net chases a bird for three or four minutes, it may suddenly drop dead from exhaustion. A safer method is to use two or three people in the aviary to catch one bird. Do not use a net when catching a larger bird, such as a parrot, from a carrying box. The best thing is to throw a towel over the bird, for once it is surrounded by darkness it will become more timid and easier to handle.

Feeding your birds

Details of the foods suitable for particular birds are given in the species descriptions, starting on page 50. This section concentrates on general diets and the practicalities of feeding your birds safely and hygienically.

Food and water containers

There are various types of food dishes and containers that you can use to feed your birds, including earthenware, glass, metal or plastic. Use a metal container for birds with strong beaks, such as parrots. They are likely to destroy any flimsy dishes and may swallow the fragments they have chewed off. A heavy earthenware bowl is advisable for nectar feeders, such as lorikeets, and some softbills. These birds tend to tip their bowl up every day, scattering the contents over the floor, and the extra weight of an earthenware container should prevent this happening. Plastic dishes and glass tube dispensers with plastic spouts are fine for smaller seedeaters.

Nectar feeders are not only messy when eating, but they also tend to bathe in their food dish. To prevent this, place a piece of wire grid with a mesh size of 5cm(2in) over the bowl; this will enable the bird to eat but not bathe.

It is vital to provide the correct size and style of water dish for your birds, an oversized water dish, for example, can result in your birds drowning. In a large aviary containing many small birds, there should be a shallow water dish so that the birds can bathe in their water. If the bowl is too deep and the sides are too steep, however, a bird may not be able to get out and, when realizing this, panic and drown.

Feeding routine

Once your bird is established in its new home, try to stick to a simple routine of regular feeding times, as this will offer your bird welcome stability. Most birds need feeding once a day, with the exception of seedeaters, whose full bowl can be left for up to a couple of days. If you feed your

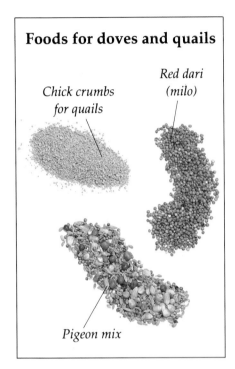

Foods for doves and quails

Chick crumbs for quails

Red dari (milo)

Pigeon mix

Above: Doves and pigeons are fed premixed seeds such as those shown above. Red dari often forms part of these mixes and can be added to feeds for other birds, such as pheasants.

Escape at feeding time

Many birds become extremely excited when it comes to feeding time. Therefore, you must be extra careful not to let them escape when you go into the aviary with the food. If your birds are the excitable type, you may find it useful to make a small flap at the front or back of the aviary through which you can slip their food in and out.

Right: This selection features the various seeds you can buy for small seedeaters. If you are a beginner, it is best to buy a premixed seed diet, but do not forget to add some cuttlefish bone.

Below: This is a typical food dish made up for softbills. It features a variety of fruit, some premade softbill diet and some livefood. Try to keep the mealworms separate from the fruit.

Foods for softbills

Mealworms

Boiled rice

Kiwi fruit

Banana

Premade softbill diet

Apple

Soaked raisins

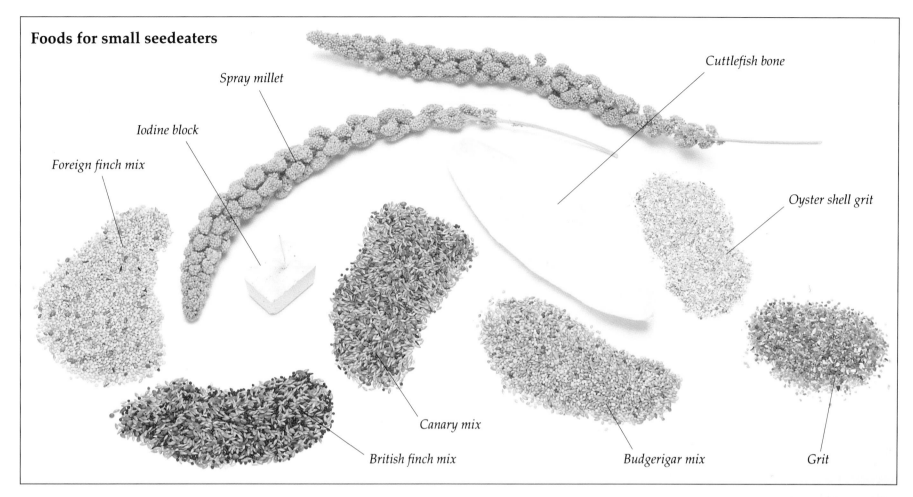

Foods for small seedeaters

Spray millet

Cuttlefish bone

Iodine block

Foreign finch mix

Oyster shell grit

Canary mix

British finch mix

Budgerigar mix

Grit

Below: An Indian blue-throated flycatcher tackles a mealworm. Given the opportunity, softbills will gorge themselves on livefood. Try to provide a variety and offer it little and often.

bird at approximately 8am in the morning, most of the food should have been eaten by midday. If no food remains at midday, then you may need to provide half as much again. If plenty of food remains in the dish, gradually reduce the amount until you arrive at the correct quantity. During very hot weather, the type of food suitable for nectar feeders will deteriorate. The best idea, therefore, is to feed them twice a day during these conditions. Try to maintain your bird's diet, once it is familiar with it. Suddenly changing it may put the bird off eating for a few days and perhaps put it off breeding.

If you do intend to change the diet, do it slowly. The best method is to mix a little of the new diet in with the food your birds are already used to, and then slowly add a bit more each day until after about a week the old diet has been transformed to the new one.

It may seem like common sense, but always check that you are feeding the correct diet for the species of birds you are keeping. Do not simply presume that you know what they eat. Always ask several different people what diet they use and this will give you a realistic idea of what to feed your birds.

Above: A plastic dish such as this full of seed is a simple way of feeding finches. Position the dish off the floor to prevent droppings from soiling the seed. This is an orange-cheeked waxbill.

15

Monitoring feeding and drinking

Monitoring your birds' feeding and drinking habits can provide useful pointers to their general health. If your birds are always eager to feed, you should have no problems, but if any of your birds suddenly goes off its food, this could very well be the first sign that something is wrong.

If your bird tends to be rather timid when it comes to feeding, which can happen when you change its diet or food dish, an effective technique is to scatter a little of the food around the dish. Continue to do this until the bird is familiar with the new food or dish. It is also important to stop bold and audacious birds inhibiting any timid birds from feeding. The most constructive way to handle this problem is to provide several water and food dishes around the aviary and so create more choice and availability for the less intrepid occupants. Since smaller birds particularly can rapidly suffer from dehydration, make sure that they have easy access to a constant supply of clean water.

Seedeaters are very wasteful, often scattering their food all over the place. It is fortunate, therefore, that this type of food does not tend to spoil. The birds for which feeding hygiene is essential are softbills, which eat a variety of different foods, and parrots feeding on pulses. With these birds, the food they eat deteriorates very quickly over a short period and so it is important to collect all the waste food from the floor each time you feed them. Otherwise, your birds may be eating food that is two or three days old, and this is obviously very dangerous. It is often a good idea to put their feeding dish inside a larger dish so that any food escaping falls into the second dish, making it easier to clean up. Any dish containing food must be under cover, as rain will ruin the food. And, of course, do not place food or water dishes underneath perches, where droppings can easily contaminate them.

Complete diets

Many diets available today are advertised as being complete diets. Many of these diets are perfectly acceptable, but it is advisable to avoid those that claim to provide substitute fresh fruit and vegetables, since there can be no substitute for these. Commercially prepared diets such as lorikeet nectar are particularly convenient and offer a safe alternative to the home-made option of mixing 10-15 ingredients together. Not only is this an extremely messy business, but bacteria could easily enter the food in the process. Complete premade diets are ideal for softbills. These ensure that they do not miss vital nutrients, but do add other foods as well.

Above: Freshly sprouted seeds are an excellent food source for budgerigars and other small parrot species. You can fix this grower to the wire mesh.

Below: The small spout on this glass tube feeder allows birds to sip the liquid nectar inside. In hot weather, replace the nectar solution twice a day.

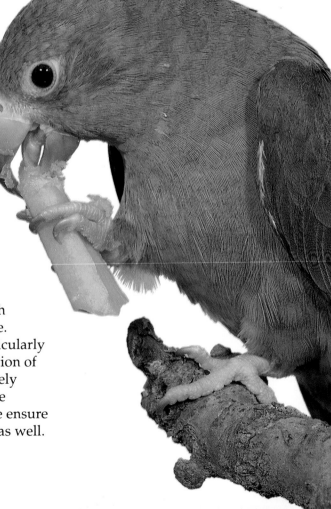

Below: It is always a good idea to feed a variety of foods to your birds. For parrots, do not chop everything into small pieces; they will enjoy chewing it up. Of course, they will make a terrible mess in the process, but this is their natural behaviour - something all birdkeepers should try to encourage.

Treats and livefood

Although birds, especially parrots, love being given treats from their owners, this is usually a bad idea. Giving your parrot a grape or your softbill some livefood is fine, but snacks intended for humans, such as crisps, contain a high level of salt and other additives that perform no useful function in the welfare of your bird.

The majority of softbills will be very eager for livefood. Try to provide this in moderation, however, for if they become addicted to livefood your birds will reject other foods and create a dangerous imbalance in their diet. In any case, it is a good idea to provide some form of mineral and vitamin supplement. Supply this in accordance with the instructions on the packet; too much can prove dangerous.

Below: As you can see, there is no shortage of foods that you can feed to parrots and parakeets; the wider the variety the better. You will find that every bird has its own favourites and will always leave some types of food.

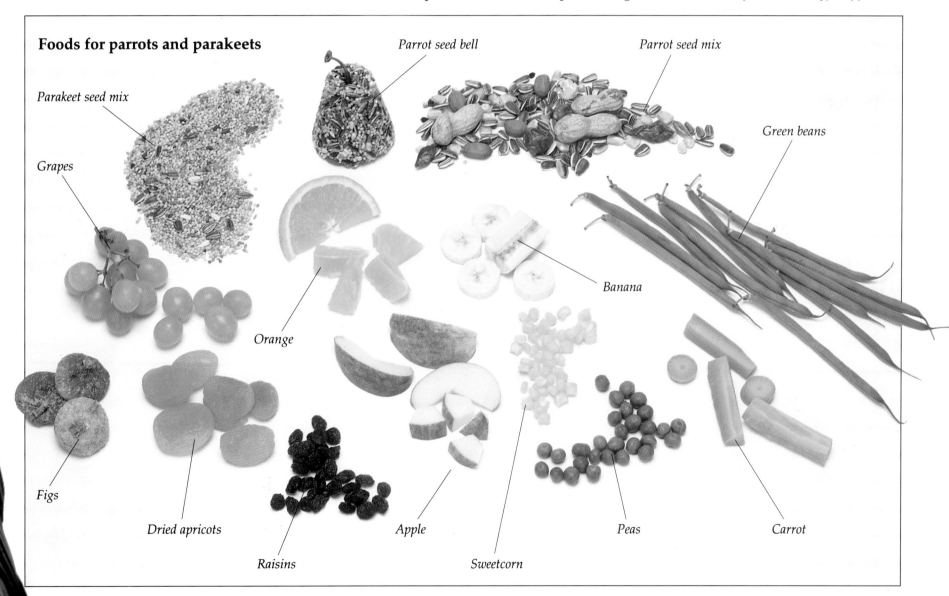

Foods for parrots and parakeets

Parrot seed bell

Parrot seed mix

Parakeet seed mix

Green beans

Grapes

Banana

Orange

Figs

Dried apricots

Apple

Peas

Carrot

Raisins

Sweetcorn

General care

The general long-term care of your birds is the most important aspect you must consider. Do make sure that you understand all your birds' requirements before you buy them.

The value of knowing your birds

It is always a good idea to get to know your birds and understand their behaviour by observing them on a regular basis. For example, you will soon get to know how they behave when they are hungry, how they respond when a stranger enters the room or how they change when they enter the breeding season. You may discover that at such times they eat more or become more active. Understanding your birds' reactions to different circumstances can be very helpful in detecting when they are ill. A bird's general appearance can also give vital clues as to its well-being. If the bird is fluffed up, for example, and looking larger than normal and is not very active, these are clear indications that something is wrong. Remember that it is better to be safe than sorry, so if you are not sure, contact your veterinarian for expert advice.

All birds need plenty of fresh air passing through their enclosure. This will help to keep the bacteria level low and thus lessen the risk of infection. Be careful, for there is a big difference between fresh air and draughts; draughts can kill. If you keep your bird indoors, it is perfectly safe to open a window during the summer months. This is not the case during cold, windy weather, however, as a draught blowing onto your bird could very well result in its death.

Establishing a locking in routine

If you keep your birds in an outdoor aviary in a climate that becomes extremely cold during the winter months, you may rest more easily knowing that your birds are locked into the back of the enclosure every night. Once you start locking your birds in at the onset of the harsh weather, it is best to continue doing so until the weather is over. Initially, you may find it difficult to coax your birds into the back of the aviary, but after a week of so they will become familiar with the routine. It also helps to have the pop hole or hatch leading to the shelter fairly high up, because birds are more likely to fly up to the entrance than they are to fly down to it. Soon you will find that when you enter the aviary at the end of the day, they will go straight into the shelter and then you can simply close the hatch. Although your birds will suffer slight stress, this should subside when they recognize the routine. It is vital to stick to the locking-in routine, for if you stop even for a few days, you will have to go

Above: As you approach your aviary, the birds will fly up to their favourite perch and sit close together, just as these Gouldian finches are doing here. If they behave differently, there may be a reason and you may need to keep an eye them.

Routine cleaning

Cleaning inside or outside enclosures is extremely important. If you keep your bird indoors, a spring clean will involve removing the bird so that you can literally scrub the cage with a suitable disinfectant and renew all the perches. If your aviary contains a sanded floor, you should rake the sand two or three times a week.

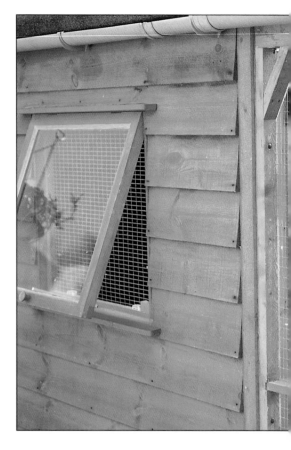

Above: You can open the windows in the shelter area on hot days or during cleaning sessions, but leave them shut otherwise to prevent draughts. Make sure they have wire mesh on the inside.

The festive spirit

One extremely important point to remember when caring for your birds is to lock them safely away on any festive occasions, especially when the deafening bangs and screeches of fireworks are likely to rend the air.

through the same learning procedure as in the initial week, and this will cause your birds unnecessary stress. Always lock your birds in during daylight hours; a window in the back shelter will help to make it more inviting. Do not attempt to lock them in at night, as they are likely to panic, fly straight into the wire and injure themselves. The best time to lock them away is an hour before dusk.

Coping with a mixed collection

Keeping many different species of birds in one aviary is not always as easy as it seems. You can often mix quite diverse species, but this is normally more straightforward out of the breeding season or with single birds. The breeding season is an important factor to consider. Once it begins, the different species of birds that once lived so happily together can suddenly turn on each other as they fight for territory and protect their nestsites. Quite literally, warfare can break out. Keeping one single bird in an aviary with several other pairs should present no problems, but if you decide to pair it up, keep a close eye on it in case trouble starts. Because the individual characters of each species vary so much, it is very difficult to give detailed advice on what species of bird you can safely keep together. (The text describing each group of birds, starting on page 50, does reflect the 'character' of each group where possible.)

The majority of birds usually moult just after the breeding season. Do not be alarmed that during the moulting period, they may not be able to fly quite as well as they usually do; this is quite normal.

Maintaining the water supply

During the winter months in temperate climates, the water bowl kept in an outside enclosure is certain to freeze over. When you arrive first thing in the morning and see the layer of ice in the bowl, do not simply break the ice, as it will quickly freeze over again. The best approach is to empty the bowl completely of ice and water and refill it with fresh lukewarm water, as this will prevent it freezing for at least a couple of hours. And never assume that the water will not freeze again until that evening, as you will probably need to replace it again after lunch.

Providing bathing water

Allowing your bird to bathe occasionally is a good way to keep it healthy. It is not sensible to provide a permanent dish for bathing unless you are prepared to change the water every day. It is essential to change the water because your bird will not be able to distinguish between drinking and bathing water and will end up drinking from the water it has just bathed in. A good method is to introduce a large, shallow container full of water into the cage or enclosure once a week and remove it after a couple of hours.

Below: A simple way of preventing birds from becoming waterlogged or drowning in a water dish is to add marbles or clean stones so that they can drink but easily climb out if necessary.

Adding new birds

If you want to add new birds to your collection, spring is the best time to do it. During the warm summer months that follow, the new birds can familiarize themselves with the garden, the aviary, the diet, their fellow occupants, etc., so that by the time winter approaches, they should be fully acclimatized. Many birds can cope with cold conditions, but it all depends on how fast the winter materializes. If freezing conditions arrive suddenly, you may lose all your birds in one go, but if winter approaches gradually and you keep your birds in a well-sheltered aviary, in general and depending on the species involved, they should be able to cope. It is not low temperatures that normally kill birds, it is the combination of wetness and wind. If your birds become wet and are in a draught, they will rapidly lose heat and die.

Basic health care

If you are new to birdkeeping, it can be very difficult to detect when a bird is ill. The signs that usually prove to be good indications are fluffed up feathers, slightly drooping wings, unwillingness to eat and general inactivity. As you become more experienced, you will be able to assess your bird's health by looking at its eyes. In a healthy bird, these should be bright and alert. If you discover any difference, you should consider calling out your veterinarian.

You may find that during the winter months, a bird kept outdoors may look rather dispirited. You may be undecided about whether to bring it into the warmth of the house or leave it for another day. If you bring the bird in, you may find it very difficult to introduce it back into an outside aviary after its spell of recuperation inside. Once acclimatized to the warmth, the bird will experience a great shock as it feels the cold again. In fact, it may be best to wait until spring arrives. With this possibility in mind, it is always useful to have some sort of indoor environment available so that when you experience a problem outside, you will have somewhere to transfer your birds without delay.

Above: A bird with a swollen and discharging eye is ill, and needs prompt veterinary treatment. Such conditions can be cured if caught in time.

Below: Typical signs of ill-health; the eyes are dull and half-closed, the wings are drooping, and the feathers are fluffed up rather than flat and sleek.

Using a hospital cage

If your bird suddenly becomes ill, you will find it very useful and reassuring to have a hospital cage standing by. A hospital cage is simply a customized cage where sick birds can recuperate. They usually consist of a wooden or metal box with one side made of glass or wire mesh. The difference between this and a standard cage is that it is fitted with a heating system, usually in the form of a low-wattage infrared lamp fixed to the roof or a number of light bulbs under the floor. The aim is to provide a stable environment with easily controllable heat where you can place a sick bird to recover in peace. The main objective is to lower the bird's stress level, so under no circumstance should you attempt to heat the bird up too quickly, as this in itself will cause a great deal of damage. It is not uncommon for a bird to recover extremely quickly during a spell in a hospital cage, so be sure to keep an eye on it and, most importantly, make sure it has a constantly available supply of clean water. If a bird does recover quickly, do not be tempted to put it straight back into its usual quarters; keep it for a few more days in the hospital cage.

Worming and dusting your birds

Your birds will need worming once, if not twice a year. Once a year is fine for birds kept indoors,

Always be prepared

It is always a good idea to have a few practical health aids standing by. These should include an antiseptic spray in case your bird injures itself, a hospital cage, another cage set up in a quiet part of your house where you can transfer any of your outdoor birds throughout the winter, and a 'pick-me-up powder' to sprinkle on food that will help your bird back to health. And, of course, always have the telephone number of your local veterinarian to hand.

but for birds kept in an outdoor aviary, where they could be in contact with wild birds, twice a year is essential. The best time to worm your birds is two months before they are due to breed and/or just after the breeding season. If you worm them during the breeding season, they may stop incubating the eggs or abandon their chicks. Worming can also affect the fertility of the eggs. Various products are available, but if you are a beginner it is best to seek advice from your local veterinarian on the most suitable one for your birds and how to administer it.

At some stage you will need to dust your bird to remove any feather mite or lice that it may have contracted. You do not need to dust birds on a regular basis, although you should check them frequently. Suitable dusting powders are available from your local pet store or veterinarian. When dusting your bird, pay particular attention to the areas under the neck and under the wings.

Keeping a parrot healthy

If you have, or you are planning to keep a parrot, it would be a good idea for you to become aware of the various diseases associated with parrots. To reduce the likelihood of problems arising from the outset, be sure to buy your bird from a healthy collection or from someone who has a good reputation for keeping birds at a high standard.

One possible problem with parrots is obesity. A good variety of seeds, nuts and fruits offered in moderation will keep your bird fit and healthy. The key words here are 'in moderation', because you must be careful not to overfeed your bird. An obese bird is prone to heart attacks and can experience various other problems. Occasionally, you may come across a bird that seems to eat very little but still puts on sufficient weight; it is this type of bird that you should keep an eye on in terms of feeding strategy.

Above: Providing a little extra heat for an ill bird can help it recover. Use a hospital cage or position a suitable heater near the cage. Be careful not to bring it too close to the bird and avoid putting the recovery cage in too small a room that may heat up too quickly; too much heat can cause further problems.

What to do if your bird seems unwell

Fluffed up, looks ill:	Bring into a warm area. Call the veterinarian if no improvement.
Heavy breathing:	May be under stress. If lung problem, call your veterinarian.
Diarrhoea:	Call your veterinarian.
Small cuts and abrasions:	Use a wound powder or antiseptic spray on affected area.
Evidence of worms:	Worm your birds once a year. Ask your veterinarian for advice.
Mites:	Dust bird with recommended flea and lice powder.
Claws catching:	Probably too long; cut them or consult your veterinarian.
Feather loss:	May be in moult. Possible feather mite; if so, dust with powder.
Broken leg or wing:	Call your veterinarian immediately.
Suddenly ill when about to lay an egg:	Bring into a warm area of 24-29°C (75-84°F) and call your veterinarian.

Nail and feather clipping

Most birds will need their nails clipped at some stage, although it is difficult to say how often because it depends on the individual bird. Parrots need clipping on a regular basis once or twice a year, while softbills may need clipping only once every three or four years.

How to clip the nails safely

Nail clipping is a delicate procedure and can be dangerous. Before you make your first attempt, ask a veterinarian or an experienced birdkeeper to show you how to carry out the procedure correctly. Once you have caught your bird, it is a good idea to have someone else hold it as you clip the toenails. If you examine each nail before clipping it, you can usually see how far the blood supply runs down the inside of the nail towards the tip. Where the blood supply is not visible, perhaps because the nail is dark, this is when common sense and experience are vital. Carefully clip one nail at a time, removing just the very last portion and leaving a margin of one or two millimetres from the cut edge to the blood vessel inside. It is always better to remove too little than too much.

If a bird has very long claws that have obviously not been cut for a year or more, you may need to cut the nails several times over the course of a year before they reach the required length. You cannot transform an excessively long claw into a very short claw with one cutting session, because you are likely to cut through the blood vessel and cause considerable bleeding. Once the tip of the nail has been removed, the blood vessel inside will shrink and you will be able to remove more of the nail after about six weeks.

If you cut through the blood supply, the bleeding can prove to be extremely difficult to stop. You can stop a small amount of bleeding by placing a little cotton wool over the end of the claw for a few minutes. If the bleeding stops, release the bird back into the aviary but do not remain close to it; this can stress the bird and thus raise its heartbeat and blood pressure so that the bleeding starts again. If there is excessive bleeding and you have failed to stop it, it is vital that you contact your veterinarian. Just to be on the safe side, however, even if you are experienced at clipping nails, it is advisable to have a coagulant, such as a styptic pencil, close at hand.

Feather clipping

The two most common reasons for clipping your bird's feathers are to restrain its flight and to prevent it flying altogether. You may like the idea of keeping birds such as ducks or pheasants at liberty in your garden, but if you buy and release them without clipping their

Above: In most cases it is difficult to see where the blood supply runs in a bird's claw, but here it shows up very clearly. Use this as a guide to how much of the claw you can safely clip away.

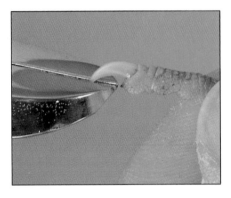

Above: Hold the toes firmly but gently to prevent the bird making a sudden movement that may cause you to cut off too much. Just cut the tip off each nail using a sharp pair of clippers.

Below: Pulling the wing out like this will not harm your bird - in this case a budgerigar - and will enable you to see the primary and secondary feathers clearly. Hold the wing out by the outer primaries, because these will not be cut.

Letting it down gently

A word of warning; if your bird has been used to flying, it is very dangerous to clip one wing and then put it straight back onto a perch. The bird will naturally think that it can still fly and jump off the perch. Without the power of flight, it will fall to the floor and could injure itself. The best approach is to clip half the required number of feathers from the wing and return it to the floor of the aviary. Hopefully, it will attempt to fly from the floor and discover that it cannot. After a few days, remove the remaining feathers (except for the outer two or three) and leave the bird a few days to get its bearings.

wings, they will disappear. The most practical option would be to clip their wings, and by the time they have moulted and the new feathers have appeared, your birds should be familiar with their surroundings and, if they are contented, you should have no problems keeping them on your premises. This approach is not advisable with parrots or any other expensive birds.

The correct procedure for clipping feathers is to remove nearly all the primary and secondary feathers - the longest feathers - from one wing. The object of clipping only one wing is to unbalance the bird so that it will only gain lift on one side and thus be unable to fly. If you clip both wings you will discover that the bird will still be able to fly. It is important to leave two or three outer feathers, so that the bird still looks neat and attractive when it closes its wing.

If you stretch out the bird's wing, you will see several layers of feathers. There are approximately 10 primary and 10 secondary feathers. The primaries are the longest feathers, and these are further away from the bird's body than the secondaries. When the time arrives it is best to have someone to help you by holding the bird and gently stretching out the wing as you remove the feathers carefully one by one. Your bird will suffer no pain whatsoever, as there is no feeling in the feathers. If you feel unsure about this procedure, your veterinarian will clip the wing for you.

The effects of feather clipping only last until the next moult, when completely new feathers will appear. If you wish your birds to have permanently clipped wings, you may have to clip the feathers two or three times a year. But do not become complacent; check your bird every month to see if the flight feathers are growing back. Complacency could easily lead you to lose your bird.

An important point to watch out for when clipping wings is to avoid touching the blood feathers. These are feathers that are still growing and so have blood continuously being pumped into them as they develop. Quite often you will find that half a blood feather will be out of the quill and the other half will still be wrapped in a silvery skin. If you come across such a feather, take great care not to cut it as it will bleed profusely.

A cure for bullying

Clipping the wing can also solve the common problem of one bird dominating and bullying another, as might be the case at the start of the breeding season if the male comes into breeding condition before the female. By clipping the male's wing, you are impeding it from flying after the female and harassing it.

Below: Ask someone to hold your bird while you clip one of its wings. Clip each feather one at a time using a pair of sharp toenail clippers; do not use scissors because the long blades are liable to cut into other areas. Cut each feather under the next one so that the clipped edge is hidden. Leave the outer two or three primary feathers intact.

Catching an escaped bird

Before considering how to catch an escaped bird, it is worth stating the obvious that 'prevention is always better than the cure'. This offers little consolation to distressed owners, however, and so these guidelines may help prevent the problem arising in the first place.

Preventing an escape in the first place

If you keep your bird inside your house, do not open the door of the cage without first making sure that all the windows and doors of the room are securely closed. If you are introducing a bird into an outside aviary, always release the bird from its box while you are inside the aviary. Do not take the bird out of the box by hand, carry it over to the aviary and then release it. It is also a good idea to have a safety porch in an outside aviary. This basically means having two openings to the aviary; the first leading into an enclosed area that has a second door opening into the aviary. By closing the outer door before opening the inner door, there is no opportunity for the birds to escape by flying over your head to the outside.

Do not panic

If your bird escapes, do not panic. Once a bird escapes, it becomes frightened and panic-stricken itself and if you suddenly start to chase it around with a net, the only thing you will achieve is to drive it further away so that it will not be able to find its way home. The best procedure is to wait for the bird to settle in a nearby tree and familiarize itself with its new surroundings. Then place some food in the aviary, leave the door open and then disappear. Before long, the bird will become hungry and return to its aviary. This method is obviously not possible if you keep a number of birds in one aviary.

If the escaped bird is accustomed to living with another bird, you may increase the likelihood of catching it by placing the cage in the garden with its mate inside. This is not a good idea if the mate is a very timid bird that is likely to scream when it is placed outside in unfamiliar surroundings. In this case, it will give off distress calls that are exceedingly likely to chase the other bird further away.

If you have an escaped bird and you also keep a dog or a cat, it is best to keep your pets inside as often as possible. This is because although you may think that your bird is used to the dog or cat, it is only used to seeing them from the safety of its cage. An escaped bird

Getting professional help

If you have tried the various methods for catching an escaped bird and all have failed, you should consider contacting a professional bird catcher, who will use a mist net. You may find that you will need to seek permission from the local authorities to allow someone to use a mist net on your property. Therefore, be prepared for some organization and possible complications.

If your bird does escape, report the incident to your local police immediately, because very often people will report sightings of unexpected birds. This may lead you to try catching your bird from various gardens, but be prepared for it to take a few days.

A soft light-proof material will cause less stress to the birds

Above: This is the safest type of net you can use to catch a bird. The net is deep so that once the bird is inside there is enough material for it to fold over the rim and prevent the bird from escaping.

Make sure that the net has a padded rim so that it does not damage the bird as it is being trapped.

will be feeling frightened and vulnerable and the sight of your dog or cat could panic it even more and result in you losing your bird for good as it flies further and further away from home.

Trapping an escaped bird

If tempting your bird back with food and an open cage or aviary door fails, another option is to attempt to catch your bird by using a trap. A good one to try is a cat trap; this is usually about 75cm(30in) long and made of wire mesh. Ideally, the bird will walk into the cage to reach some food and in the process stand on a lever that automatically closes the door behind it. The only drawback with this method is that the bird would have to be really quite hungry for it to enter such strange surroundings as a trap.

A very old-fashioned but nevertheless effective method of catching an escaped bird is the 'box-and-stick' method. This involves resting the edge of a cardboard box or wire bird cage on a stick in the middle of the garden with some food underneath it. You then connect a long piece of string to the stick, and as soon as the bird crawls directly under the box or cage, you pull the string and the box will fall down and enclose your bird. Try to make the piece of string as long as possible, because any hint of your presence will deter the bird from entering the box. Once the bird is safely inside the enclosure, slide a thin piece of wood or cardboard under it and carry the box into the aviary or inside the house. It may be old-fashioned, but it works. An important point to remember when using a trap or 'box-and-stick' method is to use the bird's usual food dish containing its typical food. Recognizing something familiar from its cage or aviary will help to calm the bird down and give you a much greater chance of catching it successfully.

Catching a bird at night

A 'last-ditch' and somewhat hazardous method of catching an escaped bird is to attempt to catch it at night. There are two very important factors to note, however. Firstly, you must know exactly where your bird is roosting and secondly, you cannot make any mistakes. You will need one other helper and a very strong torch. Ask your helper to blind the bird by shining the torch straight into its eyes, while you slowly and quietly approach (climbing a tree if necessary) and try to grab it. But beware, it is unlikely that you will be given a second chance. If you fail to catch your bird and it takes off, it could fly a very long way and only land when daylight returns. This method can work very well once you have gained some experience, but it can only be recommended as a last resort.

Above: *Keep well away from the trap and make sure that the string is tight so that you only need to give it a small tug to drop the box over the bird.*

Patience brings success

Whichever method you intend to use, you must be patient. It is rare for escaped birds to be caught straight away. The majority return to their aviaries three or four days after they have escaped. By this time they will have become hungry, making it easier for you to entice them back into their aviary or into a trap. If your bird remains in the area for the first few days, you have a very good chance of retrieving it. If there have been no sightings for five or six days, however, the chances are that it will never return.

Taming and talking

Many people always associate taming and teaching birds to talk with parrots, but the same principle applies to other species. The best way to start is to buy the most suitable bird in the first place.

The benefits of a hand-reared bird

If you are contemplating buying a parrot, for example, make sure that it has been hand-reared. The reasons for this become more obvious once you consider the problems that arise with a wild bird. When you buy a bird that has been collected from the wild, the chances are that it was snatched as a youngster or trapped as an adult bird. Either way, the bird would have suffered considerable stress and shock, and by the time it reaches its destination, the bird will naturally be frightened of humans and associate them with distress. Therefore, when you buy the bird, you will find that it dislikes humans, and this is certainly not the best way to start out. In fact, this bird will be very difficult, if not impossible, to tame.

Dealing with a hand-reared parrot is a completely different situation, because as far as this bird is concerned, its parents are human beings. On average, it takes 14 weeks to hand-rear a parrot, and it is essential to start this process from a very young age. A parrot that has been hand-reared for 14 weeks until it is weaned should become very tame. If you can buy a parrot as young as this, you should find that it is tame from the moment you take it home. If you go to buy a bird and the owner or shop assistant tells you that the bird is hand-reared and tame, do not take their word for it. The best way of testing this is to put your hand in the cage. If the bird bites you, there is no way that it is tame. And remember, a bite from a parrot hurts a lot less than paying for one that cannot be tamed.

Taming a parrot in a cage

As with many aspects of successful birdkeeping, taming your bird requires a great deal of patience; do not expect results within a few days. Try starting off by offering the bird little titbits of its favourite food through the cage, but do not be alarmed if it initially backs away from your hand, because this behaviour is very common in wild birds. After a week or so, you should find that the bird will take the food from your fingers. After a few weeks, it should be safe for you to put your hand inside the cage without being bitten. Once you reach this stage, put both hands in the cage with the hand furthest away from the bird containing some of its favourite food. This situation coaxes the bird into stepping onto one hand to reach the

Above: Use a bird's favourite food to tempt it onto your fingers. Keep your hand still the first time you do this. You will need to do this many times before you can move around with the bird.

Some birds become tamer

In a large collection of birds kept in an aviary, it is common for one bird to become noticeably tamer than the others. In fact, you may discover that such a situation helps to calm any new arrivals that you may introduce into the same aviary.

food in the other. If you continue with this technique, slowly but surely your bird will become tame. To ensure that a parrot remains tame, handle it as often as possible. As your bird grows older, it may start to nip occasionally. Every time it does this, gently tap it on the beak and tell it off.

Taming birds in an aviary

Taming a bird kept in an outdoor aviary basically involves the same approach. The best way to tame softbills, for example, is to offer them livefood; they will do practically anything for such a treat. Taming your bird, even to a modest degree, can result in lowering the stress level. If your daily routine keeps you very busy and you rush around much of the time, it is very important to slow down when you are close to your bird. Otherwise, you will achieve exactly the opposite effect of the taming process. As with any new arrivals, always enter the aviary calmly and slowly. In this way, your new bird will gradually become acquainted with you and possibly with any pets that wander around the garden.

Teaching your bird to talk

It is possible to train many species of bird to talk. The most obvious are members of the parrot family, but other talking birds include mynahs, jays and crows. If you are looking for a talking bird, it would be best to buy a parrot.

If it is kept indoors, the best method of teaching your bird to talk is to put the cage near the telephone. The first words that your parrot will speak will be the words that it has heard most often. Therefore, it will soon learn how to say 'hello'. If you wish to progress onto longer, more complicated words, repeat them over and over again and, as before, be prepared to be extremely patient. Remember that a large parrot, such as a macaw, has the equivalent intelligence of a four-year old child, and you should treat it as such.

At some time or other, you may hear a sudden screech from your bird's cage. Do not be alarmed, for there is nothing physically wrong with it, it is simply seeking attention. Once it has your attention, it will stop screaming. In fact, you can use the bird's urge to seek attention to help you teach it how to talk. After your bird has just learned to say 'hello', ignore it for a while, then as soon as you hear it say 'hello', go to it and talk to it and reward it with a piece of its favourite food. If you stay with the bird, it will stop talking because it has your attention. Then disappear around the corner, start repeating 'hello' and as soon as your bird says it, come back and reward it again. If you continue this routine, your bird will soon grasp the idea of it all. Every parrot species is capable of talking, but there is no guarantee of success - it all depends on the character of the individual bird and the dedication of the trainer.

Above: Large parrots, such as this splendid Moluccan cockatoo, are intelligent and can be tamed with patience. This species is noisy and destructive - not an ideal house pet.

Breeding but not tame

It is important to remember never to introduce a tame bird to a mate if you want it to remain tame. This is because you will always take second place to the mate. If the birds breed, then your bird will almost certainly turn against you and the tame bird you once owned will be gone forever.

Below: Teaching a parrot to talk can take a long time. It will help to have the bird around the house with you because it will hear lots of talking and stand a better chance of picking up a few words.

Breeding your birds

Below: This is a good example of the sort of nest many softbills build. You can see why they require dense foliage in which to build them. Once they start nesting, do not disturb the birds.

As with other aspects of birdkeeping, the foundation for successful breeding is to buy the right stock in the first place. Never presume, for example, that your birds are a pair; have them scientifically sexed first if you choose species in which the male and female look alike.

Buying and conditioning your stock birds

Be sure to buy your stock from a well-known source, either a reputable breeder or someone who has been recommended to you. The time spent selecting good stock and paying that little extra is well worth it, because it will save you so many problems later on.

Once you have obtained good stock, you must be sure to feed them properly. This involves obtaining the best-quality feed and making sure that they are not needing for anything. With good, unrelated, well-fed stock, you are on the way to breeding success.

Preparing for the breeding season

Privacy is paramount. When the nesting period approaches, do not disturb the birds more than is necessary to monitor their progress. If you constantly peer into the nestbox, use the lawnmower close to the birds, let the cat or dog interfere with them, etc., this will put the birds off breeding.

Birds that have been in your collection for a few months are more likely to breed than newcomers, simply because they are settled in and familiar with their surroundings. Therefore, do not expect new arrivals to begin breeding, even if it is the right time of year; they need time to become acquainted with all that is new to them.

As soon as the breeding season arrives, keep a discrete eye on your birds' behaviour so that you know what to look out for during future breeding seasons. This is very important, as you might experience certain problems at this time. For example, it is not uncommon for the male to come into breeding condition before the female. If this happens with a pair of parrots, the male is quite likely to attack the female, in some cases, extremely ferociously. In other cases, as with softbills, the male may chase the female around the aviary and this can result in her death. Clearly, learning about your birds' breeding behaviour is essential.

When they begin to lay, the majority of birds will need extra calcium. Without help, a female laying many eggs can exhaust herself. You can provide extra calcium as a powdered food supplement or by placing a cuttlefish bone in the aviary. Once your birds begin to lay, you will realize that it is not necessary to look at the eggs every day; there will be very little change from one day to

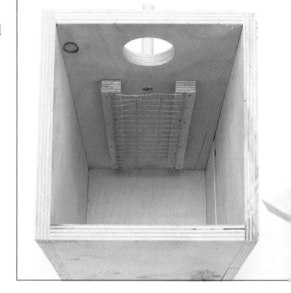

Above: This view shows the inside of a typical parrot nestbox with the roof removed. A small entrance hole just large enough for the birds to get through helps them to feel it is a safe place. A mesh ladder running down the inside allows easy access, so the birds are less likely to jump in on the eggs.

A selection of nestboxes and baskets

A budgerigar nestbox

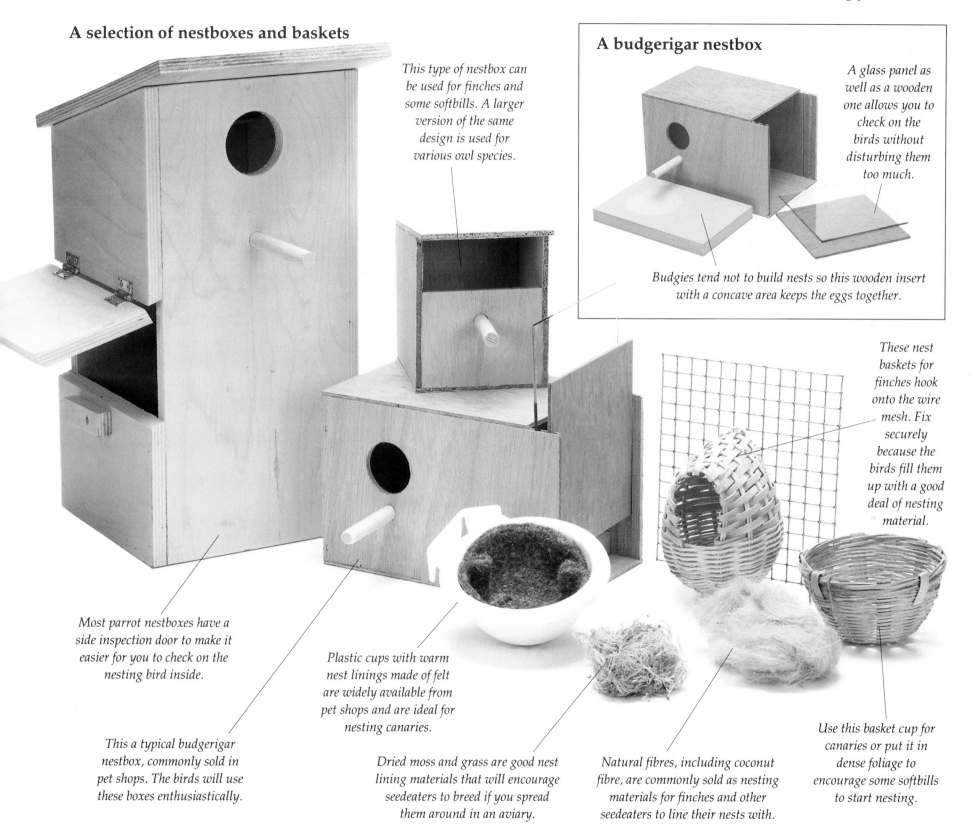

This type of nestbox can be used for finches and some softbills. A larger version of the same design is used for various owl species.

A glass panel as well as a wooden one allows you to check on the birds without disturbing them too much.

Budgies tend not to build nests so this wooden insert with a concave area keeps the eggs together.

These nest baskets for finches hook onto the wire mesh. Fix securely because the birds fill them up with a good deal of nesting material.

Most parrot nestboxes have a side inspection door to make it easier for you to check on the nesting bird inside.

Plastic cups with warm nest linings made of felt are widely available from pet shops and are ideal for nesting canaries.

This a typical budgerigar nestbox, commonly sold in pet shops. The birds will use these boxes enthusiastically.

Dried moss and grass are good nest lining materials that will encourage seedeaters to breed if you spread them around in an aviary.

Natural fibres, including coconut fibre, are commonly sold as nesting materials for finches and other seedeaters to line their nests with.

Use this basket cup for canaries or put it in dense foliage to encourage some softbills to start nesting.

Above: This is the view into a budgie nestbox with the end panel lifted up; the chicks here are about a week old.

Coping with egg-binding

Egg-binding is a serious and common problem. This is when the female tries to lay the egg but her vent will not relax enough to let the egg through. This usually happens when the weather is too cold or with a female that has never laid before. If the bird finds it impossible to lay an egg, it can kill her. The good news is that the problem can be rectified if caught in time. If you find your bird looking ill in the nestbox or lying on the aviary floor and you can feel that she contains an egg, act immediately. Firstly, place the bird in the warm (24-27°C/75-80°F). Then gently oil the bird's vent with liquid paraffin or other suitable lubricant - a small soft brush will help. This should enable your bird to lay the egg within a couple of hours. If you have no success, call your veterinarian.

the next. It is best to make a note of when the eggs were first laid and then check them approximately once a week. If you fail to register this date, you are likely to find yourself becoming increasingly impatient for the eggs to hatch. It is a good idea to make a note simply so that you know what to expect and when.

Once the chicks have hatched out

Once the chicks have arrived, make sure they have plenty of food. Young chicks eat vast amounts; in fact, you may need to double the amount of food you normally feed to your adult birds. If food becomes scarce, it is quite common for birds to kill their young or stop feeding them. The adult birds may also stop feeding their young if you clean out the nestbox. Even if it smells rather unpleasant, leave it alone. The exceptions to this rule are lorikeets, in which the nestbox can become so foul that you will lose the chicks anyway. Therefore, after a few weeks of age, you will have to risk changing the bedding in the nestbox.

Another stage to cause concern is the day that the chicks leave the nestbox. At this age, they are not very strong and not familiar with the use of their wings. As a result, they may become cold because they are not acclimatized to an outside environment or damage themselves by flying into the wire mesh. Another possible, but easily avoidable, mishap is that a chick may drown in the water dish. To prevent this happening, either remove any deep water dishes or cover them with wire mesh so that the birds can drink but not get right in. If you think that the chicks are about to fledge (i.e. leave the nest), keep a close eye on the aviary. If they vacate the nestbox on a wet and windy day, they are unlikely to survive. In fact, keep a constant eye on the chicks, even after they have fledged, just in case the adult birds decide to breed again. In this case, the adults may start fighting with the youngsters or even keep them from their food. Therefore, during the first few weeks after fledging, be aware that something could easily and quickly go wrong.

Once you decide to remove the chicks from the aviary, take them inside and keep them somewhere warm and quiet. You will need to monitor the chicks to make sure that they are feeding properly. It is quite common for them not to feed for the first 24 hours after being taken from their parents, but once they become hungry, they will begin to eat. If you wish to incubate the eggs or hand-rear the chicks of any species, it can be done, but you must be prepared for a great deal of work.

Artificial incubation

It is possible to artificially incubate the eggs from any bird. There are usually two reasons for doing this; the parent birds may have left their eggs because they were disturbed or you may decide to remove

The importance of hygienic conditions

Observing a very high level of hygiene is essential during artificial incubation, as cross-infection in an incubator can damage all your eggs at once. Dip any eggs to be incubated into a solution of warm water and an appropriate egg disinfectant. Also use an antibacterial soap or spray to sterilize your hands before touching the eggs again.

Below: Well-insulated incubators keep eggs at a very stable temperature and produce good results. A window allows you to watch the eggs as they hatch out.

Incubating an African grey egg

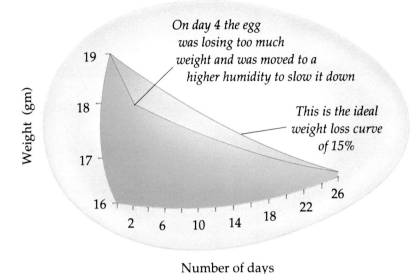

On day 4 the egg was losing too much weight and was moved to a higher humidity to slow it down

This is the ideal weight loss curve of 15%

Weight (gm)

19
18
17
16

2   6   10   14   18   22   26

Number of days

Above: This graph plots the weight loss of an African grey parrot's egg in an incubator. The egg should lose 15% of its weight until just before it hatches.

the eggs from the parents so that one pair can raise more chicks in a season. Whatever the reason for incubating eggs artificially, always remember that after incubation the chicks will have to be hand-reared, which involves a great deal of care and attention. In any case, it is important that you find out as much as possible about incubation before you even attempt to incubate your own eggs or consider buying any items of expensive equipment.

Rearing the youngsters of ground birds, such as ducks and pheasants, is generally fairly easy, but it becomes more complicated with birds such as parrots. Incubating and hand-rearing softbills can prove to be extremely difficult and should not be attempted without a great deal of experience. The safest option is to leave incubation and rearing to the adult birds.

Temperature, turning and humidity

Three factors influence incubation: temperature, turning and humidity. Of these, temperature is the most critical, so whatever type of incubator you intend using, always check your thermometer first. A thermometer does not always give totally accurate readings; for example, if it reads 0.5°C(1°F) higher than it should, it will always tend to read 0.5°C(1°F) high. To ensure that your thermometer is accurate, test it against a similar one used by someone who is successfully incubating their eggs. The majority of species should be incubated at a temperature of 37.5°C(99.5°F). Be sure to keep the incubator in a room with a stable temperature; no matter how efficient the incubator, if the room temperature varies by more than 5°C(10°F), the temperature inside the incubator will also vary.

All eggs require turning during the incubation period. Many incubators have an automatic mechanism to do this, but if you are incubating parrot eggs, you can assist the automatic process by turning the eggs by hand three or four times a day.

The final consideration is humidity. During the incubation period, all eggs lose 15 percent of their weight until a day or so before they hatch. It is vital to control this weight loss. If you are incubating eggs from birds that naturally come from a rainforest, they will require higher levels of humidity while in the incubator than the eggs from desert species. In addition, all birds have slightly different diets,

Types of incubators

Still-air and moving-air incubators are both efficient. Moving-air incubators are aimed at beginners, because the whole machine is set at one temperature. With a still-air incubator, there is a temperature gradient from the top to bottom of the machine of up to 4°C(8°F).

Candling

Throughout the incubation period, you can examine your eggs fairly easily by using a bright light and a board with a similarly sized hole cut in it. (The name 'candling' is based on the gamekeepers' original use of a candle to check the eggs of game birds.) With the light shining through it, the interior of the egg shows up enough for you to check that the chick is still alive and see how much of the egg is covered by developing blood vessels. At just over halfway through the incubation period, the veins should cover the entire inside of the egg.

Getting help from nature

The first two weeks are the most critical in the incubation period; after this, artificial incubation is much easier. Collecting eggs after the parent birds have carried out two weeks of incubation solves many problems, because the parents will have turned the eggs properly and kept them at the right temperature.

Below: When hand-rearing parrots in a brooder to keep them warm, it is a good idea to place them into plastic tubs to stop the mess they make from going all over the brooder. Putting two chicks together also helps to calm them down, and if the temperature drops too low for some reason, they will tend to huddle together for extra warmth. These are African grey parrot chicks.

which will affect the shell and, therefore, the moisture loss from the egg. This makes it very difficult to calculate the correct humidity level for each individual egg. The best way is to weigh the eggs when you first receive them and repeat the weighing process every other day throughout the incubation period. In this way you will be able to monitor and adjust the weight loss easily, making sure the loss is 15 percent. Slow down the weight loss by raising the humidity in the incubator and increase the weight loss by lowering the humidity in the incubator.

The hatching process

A day or two before it hatches, the chick breaks into the air space at the broad end of the egg. This is called internal pipping. When it is ready to emerge, the chick makes a hole in the outer shell with the egg tooth on its upper beak (external pipping). At this stage, you will need to transfer the egg into a hatching incubator. If you have only one incubator, make it as wet as possible on the inside. Before it can emerge, the chick has to rotate inside the eggshell, and if the incubator is very dry, the chick will start to dry out inside the egg and be unable to rotate, with fatal results.

It is possible to store eggs before incubating them if you keep them at 13°C(55°F) with some humidity, and turn them at least once a day. Do not store eggs for more than a week; after this you will start to lose some of them.

Sometimes adult birds have difficulty in sitting on their eggs. In these cases, it is possible to incubate the eggs artificially and then put them back under the adult birds at the point of hatch. The correct procedure is to remove the fertile eggs and replace them with dummy eggs. When the eggs are due to hatch, replace the real eggs and allow the birds to rear their youngsters.

Hand-rearing waterfowl and pheasants

When they are born, waterfowl and pheasant chicks are downy, which keeps them warm, and they are able to move about and feed themselves. (Chicks born in this condition are described as 'precocial'.) Hand-rearing these ground birds is an established and fairly easy procedure. Before starting out, it is a good idea to visit an aviculturalist who is currently rearing pheasants or waterfowl, as this will give you a good idea of what is involved. Whichever species you intend to rear, find out as much as possible about it, as this can make all the difference between success and failure.

When a precocial chick hatches, the remaining egg yolk continues to nourish it. On the first day, the chick relies solely on the yolk for energy, on the second day it will eat some of the food you put out and by the third day, much of the yolk has disappeared and the chick is feeding independently. However, do not be alarmed if at first the

Above: Using a teaspoon with the sides bent inwards is an ideal way to hand feed a small parrot chick, such as this 12 day-old cobalt-winged parakeet.

Right: Parrot chicks need feeding every few hours when they are young and the crop (a storage organ situated in the neck) needs to be filled up. This photograph shows a young chick that has just been fed and the crop is completely full. Nearly all this will disappear before the next feed time.

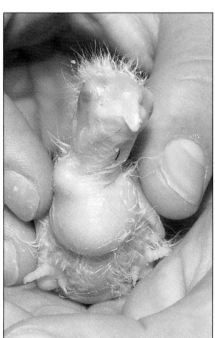

chick eats very little. These types of bird are easier to rear successfully if you keep them in small groups, because as one chick pecks, it encourages the others to feed. You could try offering them live food such as mini mealworms, but do not give them too much because the worms are addictive and the diet will soon become harmfully imbalanced. Prepared diets, such as chick crumbs, starter crumbs and pheasant pellets, are all available from pet shops.

When precocial birds are very young, you can rear them in a simple box with a heat source, such as a heat lamp, secured above them. As the birds grow, transfer them to a larger box or brooder and reduce the temperature until it reaches room temperature. After two or three months, you can keep the birds outside if conditions allow.

Hand-rearing parrots

When parrot chicks hatch, they are blind, extremely delicate and sensitive to temperature. Hand-rearing these so-called 'altricial' chicks entails a great deal of research and expert guidance. Remember that hand-rearing chicks will always be easier if you start with good-quality adult stock. If your adult birds are related, stressed or being fed the wrong diet, it is still possible for them to lay fertile eggs. If these hatch out, however, the chicks will probably not be as strong as they should be and you are far more likely to lose some to stress and disease. Begin by hand-rearing cheaper birds, such as cockatiels, and do not assume that you will successfully hand-rear an Amazon, cockatoo or macaw at your first attempt.

Be prepared for a certain amount of expense as well; not only are the birds themselves expensive, but a good-quality brooder with accurate temperature controls is essential and not cheap. If you intend hand-rearing several chicks use several brooders because, as the chicks grow, you will need to reduce the temperature in each brooder. If the chicks hatch out at one-week intervals, they will have to be kept in separate brooders at the appropriate temperatures.

When hand-rearing parrot chicks, do not reduce the temperatures too quickly. For the first few days, set the temperature at 35°C(95°F) and from day four slowly decrease the temperature half a degree Celsius every other day.

Some breeders weigh their parrot chicks every day to make sure that they are putting on 10 percent of their body weight each day. However, do not be alarmed if they actually lose weight for the first two days; this is quite common and they should begin to gain weight by the third day.

In the past, feeding hand-reared parrots the correct diet was a major problem and mistakes were easy to make. Today, several manufacturers produce complete hand-rearing diets to which you just add water. These are specially formulated for parrots and are reliable and easy to use.

Problems of scale

A vital point to remember is that people often have great success in hand-rearing a few birds, but find that things start to go wrong once they increase the number. If you rear half a dozen chicks in a room in your house, you will most probably encounter very few, if any, bacterial problems. However, once you increase the number of birds in the house, the bacteria level will also increase and this is the root of many problems. An effective way of keeping the bacteria level down is to make sure that the room is well-ventilated but not draughty. The more chicks you keep, the more hygienic you must be.

Setting up an indoor cage

Indoor cages can vary from a single cage to a large block of small aviaries. Here, we look at options for keeping birds inside.

Indoor cages

If you keep a single bird in a cage inside your house, you will probably buy the cage from a pet store. You should have no difficulty finding a cage of the right size for your bird, but always buy as large a cage as possible. Make sure that the mesh is the appropriate size. For example, the mesh in a cage for finches should be no wider than 1cm(0.4in) across, otherwise the bird may escape.

If you intend to keep a parrot, be sure to put a secure catch on the door, preferably a padlock. Parrots are one of the more intelligent species of birds and after playing with a catch for many hours, they will learn how to undo it.

For many types of bird, it is best to keep the cage in a spot where there is very little, if any, disturbance, such as a spare bedroom or a dining room that is only used occasionally. Birds thrive in stable conditions and a noisy party can upset your livestock. It is especially important to provide a quite place for small seedeaters that are breeding. The living room is fine for budgerigars and other parrots that relish human company, but avoid keeping birds in the kitchen, where cooking and fuel fumes can be a health hazard.

Heat and light are also key factors to consider when keeping a bird indoors. Here again, it is advisable to avoid the kitchen, because the changing temperatures will imbalance the bird's biological time clock and it may moult at the wrong times. Keeping your bird in a dark room will also discourage it from breeding, as the lack of light will make the bird think it is winter. If you have no alternative but to keep the cage in a room with little natural light is available, make sure that the bird receives 12-14 hours of artificial light every day.

Below: This cage is fine for keeping a single pet bird, such as a budgerigar. The elasticated cover around the bottom third of the cage prevents seeds, husks or any other mess falling onto the floor.

Place the bird in a corner or at the side of a room where it can see what is happening and also has the security of at least one wall behind it. Never place the cage on a stand in the middle of the room, as the bird will feel vulnerable from all sides and become stressed. The correct height for the cage is just below your eye level. The bird will feel more secure if it is at the same level as you are and you will find that its reactions improve when you are teaching it to speak. If the cage is on the floor, people approaching it can prove to be an extremely daunting experience for the bird inside.

Remember that your bird will make a mess in, and possibly around, its cage. You can help to prevent this by screening the back and/or sides of the cage. Mynah birds are probably the messiest birds to keep in the home, as they not only throw their food around, but also have the unpleasant habit of spraying their waste matter in all directions. In cages designed for mynahs the back, sides and half of the roof are covered in an easily cleanable painted metal.

If you keep many birds in one room in your house, you will undoubtedly have a dust problem. To reduce the dust level as much as possible, open a window in the room without creating a draught or allowing the temperature to fall too low. This will also reduce the level of bacteria. Keeping just one parrot in your house will also produce a lot of dust and you may find that a member of your household is allergic to it; this is not a common problem, but it has been known to occur.

Indoor aviaries

Rather than keeping just one bird in a cage, you may decide to set up a block of small aviaries. Each of these aviaries can measure 60x60x60cm(24x24x24in) and you could build up a group of 12 against one wall. Such banks of aviaries have proved very successful for breeding finches and they are also useful for housing delicate softbills and finches during the winter months if you usually keep your birds outside.

The easiest way to build an indoor cage is with mesh panels. Make each cage independent of its neighbour, so that if there are four or five cages in a row, it is possible to remove one cage without disturbing the others. The advantage of such a flexible system is that it is much easier to catch your birds and move them around and is therefore a lot less stressful for them. Indoor cages are fairly easy to build, but draw up a careful plan to avoid making mistakes. Examine an existing system before you attempt to build your own, as this could save you time and money.

If you do not want to build a cage, you will find plenty of inside cages on sale, ranging from very cheap to very expensive ones. Do not disregard the cheap ones as long as they are safe and suitable; sometimes it is cheaper to buy a ready-made cage than to build one.

Above: If you want to keep birds on a small scale and would like to breed them, a double finch-type cage like this is ideal - here home to canaries. These cages are easy to keep clean and will be fine on a shelf or on top of a cabinet.

Below: If you want to keep a medium-sized parrot as a pet, try to give it as large a cage as possible. This one is relatively expensive, but it is does look good in the home and provides your pet bird with plenty of room and security.

Setting up an aviary

The most important thing to remember when setting up an aviary for your birds is not to be too impatient. The time you spend visiting other collections, planning your own aviary and researching the species you wish to keep will ultimately reduce the chances of you making disappointing and expensive mistakes.

Planning the aviary

There are many factors to consider at the planning stage. Do you need to obtain planning permission for your aviary? What are the prevailing weather conditions in your garden? Can the aviary withstand the onslaught of rain, heat and, most importantly, cold in winter. Whatever species of bird you propose to keep, find out as much as possible about its requirements before you site your enclosure. You may discover that your chosen species requires plenty of branches or a great deal of shade or cover - all these different factors will determine how and where you build the enclosure for your birds.

You may decide to enclose and shelter a very open area of your garden by erecting a 2m(6ft) wooden fence panel. Not only will this alter the landscaping in your garden but, more importantly, it will provide security and protection for a small bank of aviaries. An approach such as this can present new alternatives. If you are in no hurry to build your aviary or are making plans for the following year, some clever planting can transform that open, unsheltered area into a peaceful and more natural-looking environment.

Remember that it is extremely difficult, not to mention expensive, to change anything once the aviary has been built. You may be quite content with your collection to begin with, but birdkeeping can become addictive, and after a while you may wish to enlarge your collection and add to your aviaries. Therefore, always construct your aviary to allow for expansion.

Other factors to consider

Compatibility will be a major consideration if you want to build up a mixed collection of species. It will have a considerable bearing on the size of the aviary, as it is only possible to mix certain species if the aviary is large enough.

Time is another essential factor when deciding on the size or number of aviaries to build. If you only have a limited amount of free time, it would be very impractical to build more aviaries than you can care for. The choice of species will also be affected by the time factor; delicate birds will require a great deal more attention

Below: Allowing plants to climb up the outside of an aviary not only helps to blend it in with the rest of the garden, but also provides shade and privacy for the birds inside. Keep an eye on plants, however; if they get too big, it can be difficult to check the mesh for holes.

Below: A well-planned aviary can form an important and attractive feature in your garden. The corner location of this aviary means that it does not get disturbed too much and the landscaping nearby echoes its circular design into the garden.

and are therefore much more time-consuming. Think carefully about the most suitable species of birds to keep and also the size and number of enclosures.

It is always a good idea to cost everything before you start. This means estimating not only the cost of the building materials, but also other essentials, such as maintenance, weekly food bills and - surprising as it may seem - the cost of the birds themselves.

Another point to remember is the availability of the species. It is very disappointing to set your heart on keeping a magnificent bird, find out all about the species, cost the essentials and build the aviary, only to find that the birds are impossible to obtain. Always check on the availability of the species by contacting local pet shops and reputable bird dealers.

Siting an aviary

Siting an aviary will require careful thought as there is nothing more annoying than having to move an aviary after it has been built.

If you are designing a new garden, build in the aviary requirements at a very early stage, taking into account servicing and expansion. Remember to choose a site with plenty of room to accommodate a back shelter. Even if you do not build it straight away, you may decide to add one later.

Discover the most common wind direction and then site your aviary so that it faces in the opposite direction, preferably so that it receives as much sunshine as possible. Sunshine and light are essential for your birds' well-being, not only because the birds enjoy sunbathing, but also because the ultraviolet rays in strong sunshine help to kill bacteria.

If you build your aviary in the summer, remember to take into account the typical winter weather conditions. For example, do not build your aviary in a dip in your garden, where it is likely to become flooded during the winter or act as a frost pocket. Placing your aviary underneath a tree may seem a good idea as it should provide shelter, but such a position is more likely to be dark and damp. The trees block out the sunshine, the dampness will produce a multitude of bacteria and after a heavy storm, the aviary will take much longer to dry out. There is also the risk that branches from the trees will damage the aviary and birds. However, carefully planted trees and shrubs can improve the appearance around the aviary and

Above: It is always a good idea to protect part of the aviary roof with plastic sheeting. Here, the design of these aviaries provides the birds with a large dry area that is warmed by the sun rather like a greenhouse.

Protection from weather

It is worth considering a permanent cover over the rear third of the aviary as a shelter from heavy rain and bright sunlight. On the other hand, you may prefer to construct a removable cover made of plastic sheeting or bamboo panels, which you can place anywhere on the aviary to protect your birds from inclement weather. The advantage of removable sheets is that during pleasant weather you can let as much fresh air and sunshine into the aviary as possible.

Above: This view from inside a budgerigar aviary shows the ideal distance it should be from the house; close enough to see the birds easily, but far enough way so that their noise first thing in the morning is bearable.

provide extra privacy, which may encourage the birds to breed successfully.

Viewing the aviary

If possible, build your aviary within view of your house. Not only will this add to the enjoyment of keeping birds, but it will also enable you to see at one quick glance if something is wrong. However, take into consideration the amount of noise that the birds can make. For example, parrots, parakeets and conures may prove very entertaining for the first couple of days, but after a few weeks you will become extremely irritated, especially with their dawn chorus. If you are planning to keep noisy birds, do not build the aviary too close to your house or, for that matter, to your neighbour's house. To avoid stressing your birds, do not build the aviary close to a road or a dog kennel. If you already keep a pet dog, you may find that your birds become used to it, but try to keep them apart, as the dog is likely to put your birds off breeding.

The aviary should also be easily accessible from the house to enable you to feed the birds and carry out regular maintenance. This may involve transporting tools and a wheelbarrow, so construct a path to your aviary to keep the rest of your garden looking presentable.

Security of the aviary

An important point to bear in mind is security. Parrot species, for example, are very expensive and, unfortunately, fairly easy to sell on the black market, so it is safer to keep them reasonably close to the house. If the area is guarded by alarms, so much the better. (Alarms will disturb your birds if they go off, but better that than losing your birds!) Guard dogs are also a good idea, but be sure to keep them away from your birds; otherwise, you will never breed them. Automatic lights are another simple security idea. They are relatively inexpensive, easy to fit and a good deterrent against both burglars and other predators, such as cats and foxes. They also provide an excellent light when you check your birds in the evening.

A design for a compact aviary with a single shelter

This scale model represents an aviary 2.75m long, 1.2m wide and 2.1m high at the highest point (9x4x7ft). Depending on its furnishings, it would be fine for a wide range of non-destructive birds, including budgerigars, cockatiels or softbills.

Build a snug shelter so that the birds like to be in there. The window makes it bright and inviting.

This safety zone will prevent birds escaping to the outside when you go into the flight area.

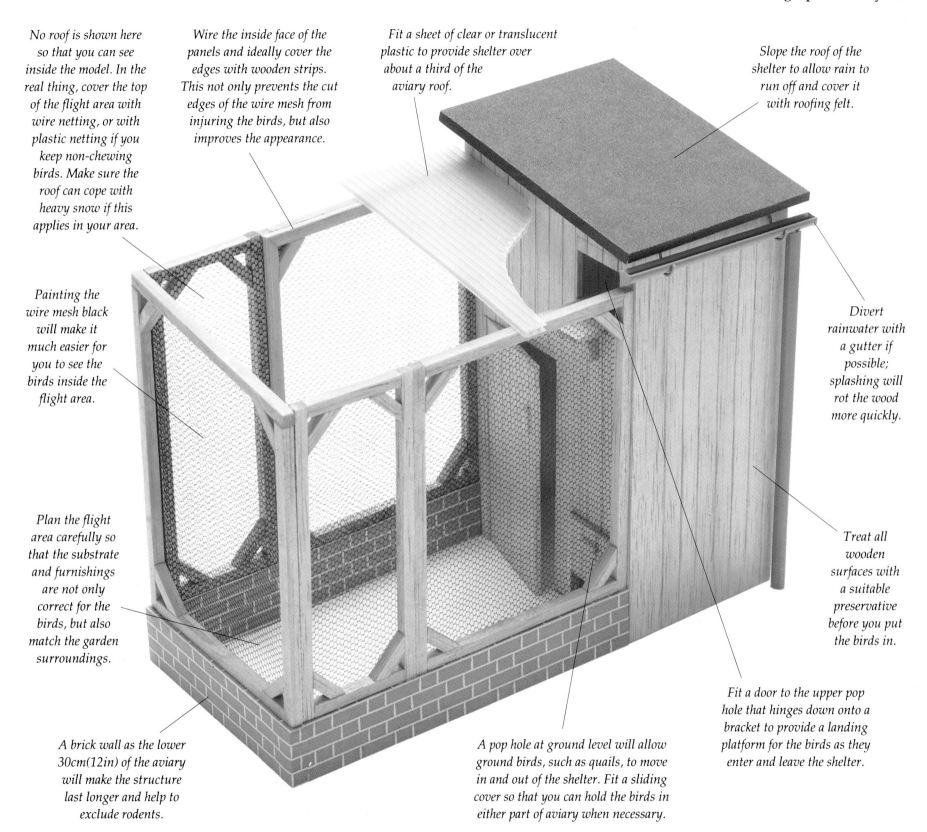

No roof is shown here so that you can see inside the model. In the real thing, cover the top of the flight area with wire netting, or with plastic netting if you keep non-chewing birds. Make sure the roof can cope with heavy snow if this applies in your area.

Wire the inside face of the panels and ideally cover the edges with wooden strips. This not only prevents the cut edges of the wire mesh from injuring the birds, but also improves the appearance.

Fit a sheet of clear or translucent plastic to provide shelter over about a third of the aviary roof.

Slope the roof of the shelter to allow rain to run off and cover it with roofing felt.

Painting the wire mesh black will make it much easier for you to see the birds inside the flight area.

Divert rainwater with a gutter if possible; splashing will rot the wood more quickly.

Plan the flight area carefully so that the substrate and furnishings are not only correct for the birds, but also match the garden surroundings.

Treat all wooden surfaces with a suitable preservative before you put the birds in.

A brick wall as the lower 30cm(12in) of the aviary will make the structure last longer and help to exclude rodents.

A pop hole at ground level will allow ground birds, such as quails, to move in and out of the shelter. Fit a sliding cover so that you can hold the birds in either part of aviary when necessary.

Fit a door to the upper pop hole that hinges down onto a bracket to provide a landing platform for the birds as they enter and leave the shelter.

Above: Although wooden aviaries look better than metal-framed ones, for large parrots you must use the strength of metal. Here, a wooden-framed aviary has been lined with metal, which would be fine for all but the largest parrots.

Above: Nailing a thin layer of wood over the frames to cover the edges of adjoining sheets of wire mesh disguises any ragged edges and prevents the birds being injured by strands of wire. It also looks much better.

Building an aviary

Before you begin any building work, make sure you know exactly where the electricity cables and water and sewage pipes are, so that you do not dig through any of them. If in doubt, go over the plans of your house and garden. If the aviary is to stand on the edge of your lawn or garden, lay down some planks or boards to protect the ground during the building process.

Never rush the building of the aviary, as this can cause you to make expensive mistakes. Examine other aviary designs and plan carefully. If you do not feel confident to do the job yourself, employ a good carpenter or buy a ready-built aviary in kit form and follow the manufacturer's instructions for assembling it.

Building the framework

Always decide what species of bird you are going to keep before you construct your aviary, as different species have different requirements. Generally speaking, a wooden aviary is more attractive than a metal one and quite suitable for, say, softbills. Wood is also acceptable for small parrots, although if they do start to attack the frame, try covering it with thin sheet metal or very fine wire. Provide plenty of perches for small parrots and parakeets to encourage them to chew the perches and not the surrounding frame.

If you intend to keep large parrots, such as Amazons, cockatoos or macaws, you will have to build the frame out of metal, as these birds will destroy any wood in sight. Even if the wood is on the outside of the mesh rather than on the inside, they will still manage to poke their beaks through the wire and demolish it. Only by lining the aviary with a thick layer of sheet metal can you stop large parrots from destroying wooden frames.

If you live in an area where heavy falls of snow are possible, you need to reinforce the aviary

Each of these flight areas measures 3m x 2.1m (10 x 7ft) and these connect with shelters that are 1.2m(4ft) square. The overall height is 2.1m(7ft). This type of aviary could be used for any non-destructive birds, including budgerigars, cockatiels, parakeets, softbills and ground birds, such as quails.

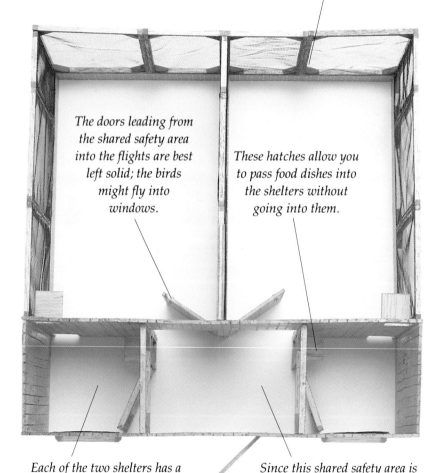

The doors leading from the shared safety area into the flights are best left solid; the birds might fly into windows.

These hatches allow you to pass food dishes into the shelters without going into them.

Each of the two shelters has a window to make it bright, and two pop holes at different levels.

Since this shared safety area is small, it is better to have the doors opening outwards from it.

No roof is shown on this model for photographic purposes, but make sure that the real thing has a wire mesh cover strong enough to withstand the weight of leaves and snow.

Plastic sheeting provides protection. Angle it so that rain water drains to the sides of the aviary.

Slope the shelter roof away from the aviary.

An overhang will help to keep rain off the shelter walls.

Avoid making the pop hole too small; about 30cm(12in) square is fine for most birds. The cover for the pop hole hinges down onto the bracket to form a landing platform. (The plastic sheeting has been cut away to reveal the pop hole simply for the photograph.)

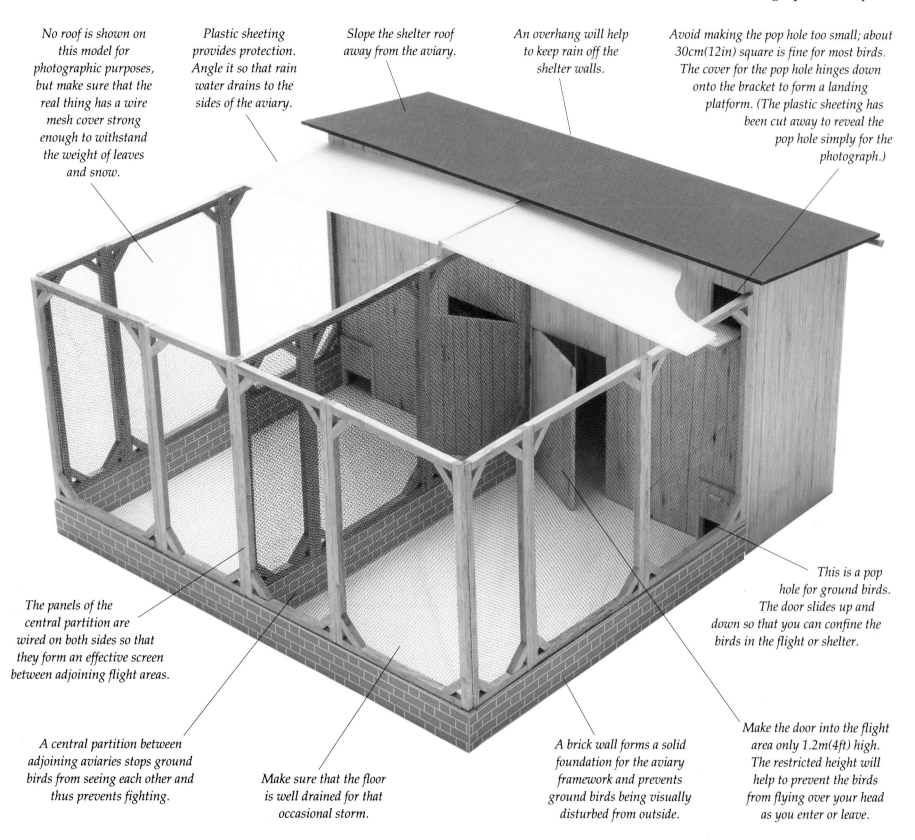

The panels of the central partition are wired on both sides so that they form an effective screen between adjoining flight areas.

This is a pop hole for ground birds. The door slides up and down so that you can confine the birds in the flight or shelter.

A central partition between adjoining aviaries stops ground birds from seeing each other and thus prevents fighting.

Make sure that the floor is well drained for that occasional storm.

A brick wall forms a solid foundation for the aviary framework and prevents ground birds being visually disturbed from outside.

Make the door into the flight area only 1.2m(4ft) high. The restricted height will help to prevent the birds from flying over your head as you enter or leave.

Ground birds

Ground birds in adjoining aviaries will spend their time walking up and down the wire trying to attack each other. This is stressful for them, so if you wish to keep ground birds in more than one aviary, either raise the framework on a low brick wall or fix a board along the bottom 45cm(18in) of the wire mesh. This will encourage the birds to breed, as they will feel more secure and relaxed if they cannot see the birds in the next aviary or other pets outside.

Below: The wooden frames of these adjacent aviaries have been built on brick wall foundations that reach a height of about 30cm(12in). This not only prevents the framework from rotting because it is not in contact with the ground, but also provides a visual barrier between the aviaries that allows ground birds to be peaceful neighbours.

framework. Even 5cm(2in) of snow on top of an aviary is a considerable burden that can cause a weak structure to collapse. You may try to overcome the problem by knocking the snow off the aviary every morning, but beware, overnight snow can really build up. Be sure to include a good drainage system in the aviary because after a rainstorm; a sanded floor will rapidly become flooded.

Selecting the correct type of wire mesh

If you keep a mixed collection of softbills, including the very small species, use very small-sized mesh, i.e. about 1-1.25cm(0.4-0.5in) across. This will also help to keep out wild birds. However, if the aviary is to house a collection of large parrots, use 5cm(2in) mesh. Remember also that the mesh should be suitably strong - often stronger than you may think is necessary. Macaws, for example, can be unbelievably strong and will slowly bend the mesh of their cage until it eventually breaks. When fixing the mesh, dig it about 45cm(18in) into the ground and continue to run it about 30cm(12in) away from the aviary to deter any digging predators. If you are faced with the problem of cats, consider installing an electric fence as well, since cats will climb over the aviary.

Access into the aviary

Remember to allocate an area for a safety porch, which is basically a double door access to your aviary that prevents birds flying straight past you as you enter. Even if you do not build a safety porch straight away, you may well decide to add one later on.

As well as a door into the aviary, it is very useful to arrange for one large panel or sheet of mesh to be easily removable. This will enable you to remove large perches from the aviary and provides easy access to the aviary for wheelbarrows, etc. If you intend including large shrubs, small trees or rocks in the aviary, place these in their final positions before you fix the mesh on.

Finishing touches

Once the aviary is built, but before you put the birds inside, coat the wood with a suitable and safe type of wood preservative. Coat any metal, including the wire mesh, with lead-free black bituminous paint, as this allows you to see your birds more easily from

Below: Squared wire mesh with apertures 1.25cm(0.5in) across is fine for finches such as this orange-cheeked waxbill and similarly sized birds. It will keep out wild birds and most mice.

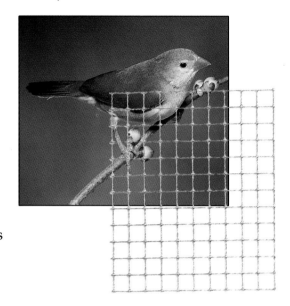

Above: For keeping budgerigars, most people use this 1.25x2.5cm(0.5x1in) mesh because it is easier to see through than the 1.25cm(0.5in) square mesh. It will keep out most unwanted guests.

Below: This sturdy 2.5x2.5cm(1x1in) wire mesh is commonly used for mixed softbill collections, which could include this emerald starling. Large areas can be used without too much framework.

Above: This robust wire mesh with holes 5cm(2in) across is used for large birds, such as Amazons, cockatoos (here, a Leadbeater's) and macaws. The wire must be very strong for macaws.

outside. You can buy some types of wire mesh that are already covered in plastic; these give the same effect as painting the mesh.

Landscaping an aviary

Once you have built the aviary, you can begin to landscape it. (Unless, of course, you have put in some plants and/or rocks before you complete the aviary structure.) You will need to consider how it will look from all angles and not just from the front; a well-designed aviary should look impressive from any angle. If the plants and shrubs inside the aviary blend naturally with the outside surroundings, you can create a very pleasing effect. Planting your aviary provides plenty of scope for your creative talents. Again, much will depend on the species you keep. Bear in mind that plants not only make the aviary more attractive, but also provide enjoyment and security for the birds in the form of perching and nesting sites.

Always remember to allocate an area for a nestbox, where the birds will be disturbed as little as possible. This could be behind a log, at the side of the aviary or, ideally, at the back of the enclosure.

Landscaping a parrot aviary

Landscaping an aviary can vary enormously depending on the species you keep. If you wish to keep parrots, you cannot have any plants or shrubbery inside the mesh, as the birds will completely destroy them. One solution is to plant shrubs and small trees outside along the sides and back of the enclosure to give the impression that the birds are in a natural habitat. If at all possible, furnish a parrot aviary with very large logs and hollow trees, but remember that these should not replace the normal perches. Cover the floor with sharp sand. A depth of 7.5-10cm(3-4in) of sand should be enough to prevent seeds germinating in the soil underneath. A sanded floor is easy to clean; simply rake it over two or three times a week to remove droppings and waste food, and completely replace the sand once a year. By positioning a group of rocks in one corner and covering them with sand you can create two or three levels, which can look very effective.

A softbill aviary

Landscaping an aviary for softbills offers many more alternatives. The floor can be covered with sand, grass, wood chippings or gravel, as well as rocks and hollow logs. Sand is not particularly attractive over a large floor area, although it is a good idea to place a little sand underneath the perches to catch the droppings and to make cleaning easier. If you like the idea of a small grass area inside your softbill aviary, you will be pleased to learn that this is not a problem, but do remember to cut the grass regularly. This may not be very easy in a

Above: To save on expensive wooden panels, you can make the partitions and doors between the safety area and the shelter or between the birdroom and shelter from wire mesh on wood frames.

Above: This is a good example of a well-planted softbill aviary that has been allowed to grow on. The thick evergreen trees provide excellent cover and nesting places for the birds and new arrivals should settle in quickly.

small aviary as you will find it difficult to manoeuvre a lawnmower and the birds will have nowhere to escape from the noise.

Wood chippings are a good practical floor covering, although you will have to replenish them twice a year by adding a few more bags and, as with the sand, completely replace them every year. Gravel is a less satisfactory option because droppings and food debris fall between the stones and are difficult to clean out. However, if you build a small pond in a softbill or parrot aviary, a zone of gravel extending 30cm(12in) around the edge will prevent the area from becoming muddy.

Rocks can greatly improve the appearance of an aviary, but remember not to place them where they are likely to become covered in droppings. Hollow logs can also look very impressive in a softbill or parrot aviary, but will obviously last longer in a softbill aviary. An effective way of creating a natural look is to stand a large hollow log upright and then fix several perches to it, giving the impression of a tree. You can make paths in the aviary from concrete stepping stones, flat rock (at the level of the lawn), sand or even gravel (but only if the birds are unlikely to make a lot of mess in this area).

Most softbills will investigate very small, new shoots, so be sure to choose large, mature plants. You may find that small plants benefit from the protection of green, plastic-coated mesh for the first month or two until they become established. Vary the size and type of plants so that they do not all outgrow the aviary at the same time.

Choosing and locating perches

It is absolutely essential to obtain the correct size of perch and fix it in the correct position. You can determine the correct size of perch by looking at the bird's feet. When it is sitting on the perch, its toenails should reach all the way round and almost touch each other. Nail the perch very firmly to the side of the aviary framework, preferably fixing it in two or three places. If the perch is fixed on the wire and is not secure, it will gradually drag the wire down and leave a hole. You can also attach perches to a post in the centre of the aviary or to the roof. If the aviary is long and narrow, place the perches at either end to encourage the birds to exercise by flying between them.

Smaller birds and some species of softbills appreciate a few springy perches on which to jump about, instead of sitting on a solid foundation. It is quite safe to provide perches with a degree of springiness, but consider their shape carefully. Avoid using sharply V-shaped branches as perches; it has been known for stressed birds to fly straight into the 'V' and be caught by the neck. Do not attach a perch on a piece of wire hanging down from the aviary roof; if a bird suddenly panics, it is quite likely to break its wing by flying into the wire. Also avoid placing perches over food or water dishes, as you run the hazardous risk that droppings will fall into the food or water.

Above: These sandpaper perch covers are useful in several ways: they are easy to replace to keep the perches clean; they give the birds an excellent grip on the perch; and they help to keep the birds' toenails short as they are rubbed against the abrasive surface.

Wooden perches for larger softbills and small parrot-type birds, such as budgies.

Plastic perch suitable for finches and small softbills.

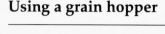

Below: Many types of perches are available for cages and aviaries. Plastic and wooden types are both suitable in most cases, but it is very important not to give plastic perches to large parrots that can chew them; the birds may break off pieces of plastic and swallow them, which can be dangerous, if not fatal. Large wooden perches are best for parrots, but since they are usually destroyed so quickly, it can be cheaper to cut natural perches from trees.

These plastic perches are suitable for many medium-sized birds.

Plastic and wooden alternatives for large softbills and parrots.

Feeding bowls

In a softbill aviary, where birds may be flying high up or perched on the ground, it is a good idea to have two sets of dishes. Change the position of the dishes on the ground as often as possible, so that no single area of the aviary becomes irreparably damaged. There are two ways of constructing the higher dishes. One is to build a welded mesh holder 1.2-1.5m(4-5ft) above the ground onto which you can place some dishes. (If you opt for this option, place some sand directly below the holder to catch any mess). The second option is to place the food dish on a wooden platform with a lip around the edge. The lip functions as a 'bib' to collect the mess left by the birds. Remember, it is very dangerous to leave old, uneaten food lying around the aviary. Fix covers about 30cm(12in) above the food and water dishes to prevent contamination from wild bird droppings and to keep the food dry.

The best place for water dishes is in the outside area of the aviary and not in the back shelter, where they can become very dusty. The dish can be very simple - a plastic bowl for softbills containing about 2.5cm(1in) of water and a galvanized metal bowl for parrots. Larger parrots, such as cockatoos, Amazons and macaws, have no difficulty in tipping over a light bowl, so fill their dish with at least 5cm(2in) of water to make it heavier. You may find that as soon as your birds are given water, they tip it out and play with the dish until they become rather thirsty in the afternoon. To guarantee a supply of water all day, give them a larger water bowl and, if necessary, place a clean rock in the centre so that the birds cannot knock it over. The only time your birds will not require a water dish is if there is a pond in the aviary. (A 'pond' here means a small, easy to clean concrete or plastic structure.) It is fine for the birds to drink from such a pond, providing you clean it out thoroughly at least three times a week.

Lighting the aviary

If you have an electricity supply running close to the aviary, you may want to give your birds extra light before the breeding season to encourage them to breed a little earlier. It is also a good idea to provide small birds with a little extra light to extend their feeding time during short winter days. And consider fitting a dimmer switch so that the birds are not plunged suddenly into total blackness. Never position lights where the birds can reach them, as this is dangerous for both birds and lights. Cover any lights inside the aviary with welded mesh 7.5-10cm (3-4in) away from the bulb. A 60-100 watt bulb per aviary is fine. Try a 5-8 watt bulb burning at night to combat 'night fright.'

Using a grain hopper

If you keep some of the more common ground birds, you may decide to use a grain hopper, at which the birds can easily peck. Be sure to replenish the hopper once a week. Before refilling it, completely clean out all the old food, otherwise dust and crushed pellets will build up and the hopper may become blocked without you realizing it.

Below: This is the sort of wooden perch suitable for an Amazon parrot. For any bird, make sure that the diameter of the perch allows the toes to go round more than halfway but not so far that they cross over each other.

Maintaining the aviary

To keep your aviary in good shape and to ensure the safety and well-being of its occupants, it is important to carry out regular inspections and a programme of general maintenance.

Treating the aviary framework

Once a year, or at least every other year, you should retreat any wood on the aviary. Some of the new wood preservatives are produced in a range of colours, which can make your aviary look very attractive if it is coated on a regular basis. There is no reason why a wooden-framed aviary cannot last for over 20 years if it is regularly painted with a wood preservative.

Before you begin to treat your aviary, make sure that the weather has been dry for 24 hours, otherwise the preservative will not soak into the wood completely. Lock away all your birds and do not let them back into the aviary until at least 24 hours after you have finished using a wood preservative.

Many people also like to paint the wire of their aviary with a black bituminous paint, as it is much easier to see into an aviary through black wire than through galvanized wire. A good coating of bituminous paint is only required once every three or four years; after that, it will slowly start to peel off. Again, it is very important to make sure that all your birds are safely locked away before you begin painting; if they come into contact with the paint, it will make a terrible mess of their feathers. If the weather is dry and bright, you can let your birds back into the aviary after 24 hours, but if it is a little damp, it is safer to wait 48 hours.

Periodic inspections

It is also very important to make thorough periodic checks of your aviary every two months. This may seem an obvious thing to do, but after a while you become so accustomed to seeing your aviary, that you do not notice that a small hole has appeared in the roof or that the frame is starting to lean to one side. Inspect the entire aviary, checking for holes, slipping perches, signs of rodents, etc.

Controlling rodents

Rodents can cause serious problems. The telltale signs of rats are the large holes in the earth that lead to their burrows. If you discover that you have rats, deal with them as quickly as possible, as they are quite capable of killing birds. Mice are less dangerous, although it is still very important to deal with them immediately. Not only will they eat the food intended for the birds, but they will also

Above: Treating a wooden aviary regularly with a suitable preservative will extend its life to 20 years or more. If left untreated, the wood will rot away in about five years, depending on the weather conditions. The wooden framework of this aviary has been stained with black preservative and is matched by the black painted mesh.

Below: To keep your birds healthy and the aviary looking smart, you will need to rake the sand or gravel at least once a week - three times a week ideally - and remove any droppings, waste food and feathers. The more birds you keep, the more cleaning you will need to do.

contaminate food and water dishes and spread disease. Once you suspect a rodent problem, you must act immediately. Mice can be easily disposed of with traps and poison. If you put down poison, place it in the tunnels outside the aviary and around the perimeter and not inside the aviary, otherwise the birds may come into contact with it. If you are not familiar with dealing with rodents, seek advice or hire someone to deal with them for you. Sensible precautions to keep them out include installing solid, rodent-proof foundations in your aviary and storing all foods in metal or heavy plastic bins.

Regular cleaning

The back or inside shelter of your aviary will require cleaning out once a week, especially during the winter months, when the birds may be locked in for up to 12 or 16 hours a day. Once a month, thoroughly scrub and disinfect the back of the aviary, replacing perches if necessary. Oil all hinges and locks every three months, whether they need it or not, as this will prolong their life up to three or four times. This will save money in expensive replacements.

Annual maintenance tasks

During the autumn, the roof of your aviary may become covered in leaves. It is a good idea to remove these, as a heavy build-up can cause the wire mesh to sag, and it is difficult to tighten up again.

After a year, the ground material in your aviary will have become soiled, so whether you are using sand, wood chippings or gravel, completely replace the material every 12 months. Furthermore, it is a good idea to freshen up any soil in the aviary by digging it over.

If you keep parrots, you will no doubt be replacing the perches regularly as they are destroyed. If you keep softbills, replace every perch in the aviary once a year, just before the breeding season. Remember to lock your birds away before you begin to replace the perches, because this procedure can prove quite stressful for them.

Just before the breeding season is also the right time to trim any overgrown plants in the aviary or, in some cases, to replace plants completely. Do not allow large plants to grow through the aviary wire, as they can easily push or pull the mesh away from the frame. Trim plants every year and keep them at least 10cm(4in) from the top of the aviary. It is also a good idea to keep an eye on the growth of trees surrounding the aviary; after four or five years, the trees may have grown to such an extent that they block out the all-important sunlight, which most birds love to bathe in.

When the cold weather approaches, do not assume that your heaters are still in working order and that the thermostats will cut in when the temperature falls below a certain level. Always check your heaters before the onset of winter to avoid situations where your birds are freezing to death while you attempt to repair the heaters.

Below: This aviary is a well supplied with good solid perches. Remember to replace all the perches - whether chewed or not - once a year. Avoid attaching perches directly to the wire; after a while a hole may be torn in the mesh.

The benefits of a birdroom

A back shelter is a small enclosed area at the back of an aviary. If you have more space available, it is sensible to set up a birdroom. Birdrooms are usually sheds connected to an outside aviary. The idea is to use part of the shed as inside quarters for your birds, so a practical design would be four or five outside aviaries, each with a compact inside area, where the birds can escape bad weather. A birdroom has several other advantages. It can function as a safety porch, so that if a bird escapes at feeding time, it will fly straight into the shed and you then have a chance to catch it before it is completely lost. If part of the birdroom consists of inside quarters for birds, it is possible to chase your birds inside and shut them in during periods of particularly bad weather. The birdroom is also a practical place for storing equipment, food, containers and, if you are fortunate enough to have a water supply and a sink, you can wash dishes and feed the birds all from this one room.

The birdroom is the most hygienic place to prepare your birds' food, as many foods can be rather messy. It also enables you to feed your birds indoors, rather than in the outside aviary. This has a number of advantages: firstly, it is easier to check all your birds at one glance as they come inside to feed and you can monitor how much they are eating. More importantly, you will only be feeding your birds and not any wild birds.

If you feed your birds in the outside flight area of your aviary and the wire mesh measures 2.5cm(1in) square or more, be prepared for visiting wild birds to eat the food intended for your birds. As well as losing most of the food, you will find yourself with a much more dangerous problem; the droppings from the wild birds can infect the food and, in turn, your stock.

Always remember to rotate the stock of food that you keep in the birdroom. If you leave food in the same container for

Below: This is a fine example of a birdroom with a spacious enclosure for the birds. With such a set-up you could keep your birds inside for long periods without problems. Even so, you should only do this if the weather turns bad: fresh air and sunshine provide the best environment for really healthy birds.

too long it will become contaminated with mites, and these are very difficult to get rid of. Establish a routine of emptying out food containers in your birdroom once a month and not refilling them with seed until you have cleaned them out thoroughly.

Rodents in the birdroom

Rodents are a common problem in the birdroom, tempted by the warm and dry conditions and the added benefit of a constant food supply. As with the wild birds, rodents are not only a problem because they eat all the food, but also because they will contaminate it and spread disease. Obviously it is a good idea to keep a supply of traps and bait on hand, but prevention is better than cure, so always keep your food and seed in sealed containers. Metal or very thick plastic bins are the only ones that will keep rodents at bay.

Inside flights

If your birdroom is large enough, you may like the idea of creating some small, completely inside flights. Here, you can overwinter any delicate birds or attend to any birds that look ill. Do bear in mind that once you have brought them inside, you may find it difficult to return them outside again until the spring.

Most breeders find it very useful to connect electricity to their birdrooms, not only to produce warmth but also to enable them to install artificial light and extend the daylight hours as the seasons change. This encourages birds to breed.

Hygiene in the birdroom

Once the birdroom has been established for a month or two, you must watch out for a rapid build-up of dust. This is mainly due to the dry conditions in the room and the handling of seed. Do remember that dust can be very dangerous, as it allows bacteria to travel around the room. When the weather is warm, the best way to overcome the dust problem is to leave the door open and allow fresh air to pass through the room, but beware of potentially deadly draughts. (Be sure to fit a wire screen door if there is any danger of the birds escaping or anything entering the room.) You can also use ionizers and air cleaners. Ionizers are readily available and will precipitate dust out of the air; do remember to clean around them occasionally. Air cleaners can be rather expensive, but if you have a large birdroom, such devices are essential.

Birdrooms can vary from a small room connected to one flight, to a large set-up connected to many flights. With a very large system, it is vital to maintain the highest standards of hygiene, because harmful bacteria spread more rapidly in the enclosed environment than in an outdoor aviary. On the other hand, if you only have a small set-up, you are much less likely to encounter such problems.

Above: This neat array of small flights housing canaries covers one wall in a well-organized birdroom. These units are very flexible and user friendly, and are not difficult to build from scratch. The room is bright and welcoming.

Above: The centre partitions should be easily removable so that you can give more space to a pair of birds or move them to the next cage without having to catch them and cause needless stress.

Above: The cage doors should be wide enough for you to reach inside to clean every part of the interior or to catch a bird when it is really necessary.

Above: The bottom of each small cage is removable so that you can clean away the droppings and waste food without disturbing the birds.

A SELECTION OF BIRDS TO KEEP

When the time comes to choose which type of bird to keep, the most important advice to follow is to go and see as many different birds as possible. By doing this you will gain a much clearer idea of the species available and whether you can offer suitable facilities in which to maintain them.

As a basic rule, the easiest birds to maintain are the seedeaters. These include many popular favourites, such as finches, canaries and budgerigars. When not kept for breeding purposes, you can safely place seedeaters with other seedeating species with only slight complications. And if you provide ample food and water in their cage or aviary, you can leave seedeaters alone a few days at a time .

Although slightly more difficult to maintain than the seedeaters, the parrot species are still relatively simple to care for. Parrots are more intelligent than the majority of other birds and so you should not leave them alone in a cage in the corner of a room. These birds demand attention and you must spend time with them; if you leave them alone, they will simply pine away.

The softbills present the most complications as far as maintenance is concerned. These complications mainly revolve around their feeding requirements, which can vary tremendously. Some species will thrive on a simple mixture of diced fruit and seed, whereas others need nectar and large quantities of livefood. It is quite possible to keep a mixed collection of compatible softbills and often this can be the best way to keep them.

Remember that any birds you keep will absorb time and expense. Do gain advice from other collectors and learn from their mistakes rather than making too many of your own.

Budgerigars

At about 18cm(7in) long, budgerigars are small enough to keep as single birds in a suitably roomy cage in your home. Cover the floor of the cage with paper and spread a layer of loose bird sand on it or buy ready sanded sheets from your pet shop; the sheets are better for your bird and easy to clean out.

If you wish to keep a large number of budgerigars, house them in an outdoor aviary. Although they are surprisingly hardy birds, do protect them from excessive rain by covering part of the aviary with transparent plastic sheeting. Budgerigars will quickly acclimatize to cold winter conditions, although, as with many birds, it is important to protect them from frost. During the winter months, it is a good idea to shut your birds in every night. Initially, you may find it difficult to persuade them into the shelter, but soon your birds will recognize the routine and present no problems.

Feed your budgerigars with a ready mixed diet or prepare a mix of three parts white millet, three parts canary seed and one part panicum millet. Your bird will also appreciate supplementary foods such as chickweed, lettuce, carrots and fruit. Budgerigars drink frugally but it is essential for them to have a constant supply of fresh water available. During the summer months, they will love being gently sprayed with a mist sprayer and are likely to drink drops of water hanging from the perches and bars of the cage or aviary.

Although budgerigars do not require a great amount of exercise, it is beneficial to let your home-based bird fly around the room a least once a week. Before letting it out of the cage, remember to close all the windows and doors, cover any open fires and remove any poisonous plants; too many people have lost their birds by not doing so.

They love to gnaw, and so budgerigars will feel at home in a cage or aviary furnished with plenty of wooden perches and maybe a cuttlefish bone. As with all birds, keep their cages and aviaries very clean by scrubbing

Right: The striking cobalt budgerigar is a rich, deep cobalt-blue, with the tail feathers in a much darker shade. The colour has come from the influence of the so-called 'dark factor' in breeding.

Grass green parakeets from Australia

Budgerigars are native to Australia, where the normal colour form is grass green. They belong to the parrot family of birds and all the various types and colour varieties produced by selective breeding share the same scientific name of *Melopsittacus undulatus*.

Left: Sky blue budgies are produced by breeding sky blues with sky blues, but after a few generations the colour will become faded and dull if the best birds are not used to breed from. If this happens, they may need crossing with green budgies to 'refresh' the colour.

Right: This male bird is a yellow-faced dominant Australian Danish banded pied, and is a good example of how far selective breeding has developed. In breeding terms, such 'show' budgies are clearly a long way from the humble pet budgie kept in the average living room.

them thoroughly once a week to remove any build-up of food and droppings that could harbour bacteria.

You can keep quite a few budgerigars in one large aviary, as these birds hardly ever fight. Unfortunately, they do not have a very long lifespan, the majority living up to seven years, but during that time they do provide many people with a great deal of pleasure and companionship.

Budgerigars are more intelligent than canaries and will often indicate this by displaying human mannerisms, such as climbing ladders and looking into mirrors. As members of the parrot family, they have the ability to talk. If you wish to teach your bird to speak, buy a young male and keep it separate from other budgerigars. Unfortunately, there is no guarantee that your bird will learn to talk or for that matter learn any tricks, but you can try.

Budgerigars will breed very readily, and are mature enough to do so at a year old. In fact, they will breed all year round if given the opportunity. It is important to prevent them from doing so because if they lay in cold weather they run the risk of becoming egg-bound, and this can kill. The best method of controlling breeding is to remove any nestboxes in late summer, thoroughly disinfect them, and replace them in the spring ready for the new breeding season. The typical clutch consists of three to eight eggs and it is quite common for five or six chicks to hatch out successfully. Incubation lasts 18 days and usually begins when the second or third egg has been laid. The chicks should fledge (i.e. be mature enough to leave the nest) approximately 35 days after hatching. In an aviary, one male bird will often mate with several different females in the colony, and so you may be confused about which adults are breeding together. Do not add any more birds to your collection during the breeding season, as this is the one time they can become aggressive.

Left: A tufted grey-green budgerigar. The tuft consists of a few feathers standing almost upright in the centre of the head. Tufted budgerigars have been bred in many colours.

Right: If you compare this spangle sky blue budgie with the sky blue one shown on page 53 you can see exactly what effect the spangling produces. Notice how the wing feathers have a pale centre and dark edging. With such a wide range of mutations and colours to choose from, it becomes clear how people get hooked on breeding new variations.

Right: *The yellow-wing dark green budgie has a laurel green body and yellow wing feathers that almost lack dark markings. Other variations include the yellow-wing light green and the yellow-wing olive green.*

Canaries

Canaries are among the most commonly kept birds in captivity. They range in size from 10 to 17cm(4-6.7in), depending on the variety. Such a size should not present many housing difficulties. In fact, a cage 40cm(16in) long is perfectly acceptable for one bird, although two birds would require a 50cm(20in) cage. A rectangular wire cage is the most hygienic. Fortunately, canaries do not make much mess, so you only need to clean their enclosure thoroughly once a week. Furnishing the cage with toys is a good idea as it averts boredom, but not to the point of overcrowding; one or two toys - replaced periodically - is quite sufficient.

Canaries are relatively hardy, and once fully acclimatized will happily live in an outside aviary throughout the year, providing they are protected from heavy rain or draughts. In fact, locating the cage or aviary in a sheltered area is vital in order to cut down their exposure to draughts.

Canaries are very easy to feed; all they require is a simple canary seed mixture, plus a little supplementary greenfood and grit for their digestion. It is quite common for canaries to live on a seed diet only, but they do benefit from and enjoy fresh greenfood. Canaries are sensitive to changes in their diet and will thrive on an unchanging feeding mixture and routine. Provide an increased amount of food throughout the breeding season.

Many people enjoy keeping canaries, not only because they are easy to look after, but also because they sing. Only the males have this ability, however. If you want to buy a canary solely for its song, choose a male roller canary, as these birds have been bred specifically for this

Island birds that have blossomed into colour

Wild canaries are dull yellow-brown birds native to the Canary Islands, Madeira and The Azores. The domestic varieties raised from the wild species by selective breeding are available in a wide range of colours and body shapes.

Right: The green border canary - and other border canaries - should have an alert, active and lively disposition. If you want to show them, they should be neither coarse nor heavily built. And of course, they must have good plumage.

Below: This remarkable clear yellow Norwich canary is a good example of one of the many types of Norwich canaries. It is the best-known variety and has been widely kept since the beginning of the twentieth century.

Right: Nowadays, the pretty red factor canary is bred by many people purely as an exhibition bird. Many years ago, canaries were kept principally for their attractive song, but now, with new colours being bred all the time, showing is often the priority.

purpose. Even though canaries can sing beautifully, they cannot perform tricks or imitate the human voice, like budgerigars. It is the cock bird's ability to sing that distinguishes it from the hen.

Another advantage of keeping canaries is that they live much longer than most other birds of a similar size. Their average lifespan is 10 years, although some have been known to live for up to 20 years. This factor, together with the convenience of their simple diet, their minimum space requirement and the fact that they pose no threat to children or strangers, explains why canaries continue to be such popular pet birds. Not surprisingly, therefore, they are particularly suitable birds for beginners to birdkeeping.

You can safely leave canaries on their own for up to two days, providing they have sufficient food and water. If you plan on being absent for a longer period, be sure to ask a friend or neighbour to check on your bird every other day.

As canaries can be rather timid birds, it is not a good idea to mix them with other birds larger than themselves or with birds that may bully them. It is possible, however, to keep a cock and a hen together, as long as you separate them two months before the breeding season begins - unless, of course, you wish to breed from them.

Canaries are not the easiest birds to breed and you may also experience difficulties in encouraging the adults to rear their youngsters. An average

clutch consists of four or five eggs, laid on alternate days. So that all the eggs hatch at the same time, it is common practice to replace a freshly laid egg with a dummy egg and then return the real eggs when the hen has finished laying. This makes it easier for the hen and achieves a better success rate. Canaries begin to build their nests in early spring and, once they have laid all their eggs, incubation lasts 14 days. The chicks fledge 14 days after hatching. Canaries are quite capable of breeding several times in one season.

Right: The roller canary is not bred primarily for its looks, but for its song. It will sing almost continuously and delivers an enchanting and melodious song. If you want a canary for company to listen to then this is the one for you. It is only the male birds that sing.

58

Above: *This very strange-looking white variegated Parisian frill canary is probably one of the more extreme varieties of canary that you will come across. There are several varieties of frill canaries, the chief ones being the Parisian, Dutch and Italian frills. 'Frill' refers to their frilled feathering. Several colours are available.*

Left: *The striking variegated buff Gloster corona canary, like all Gloster canaries, is a relatively new variety. Gloster canaries first appeared on the showbench in 1925 and have grown in numbers and varieties since then. Breeding canaries for certain looks can be very complicated and can give rise to genetic problems.*

Finches

Finches are lively and colourful birds that are universally popular because they are easy to care for and reach a small size, usually 10-15cm(4-6in). Because of their manageable size, it is quite acceptable to keep a pair of finches in a small indoor cage measuring about 60cm(24in) long and 30cm(12in) wide and deep, made of plywood or other sheet material with a front panel of 1cm(0.4in) wire mesh.

They will also live happily outdoors, but, as with all small birds, they have a large surface area compared to their body weight and so are very susceptible to changes in temperatures. It is vital to acclimatize finches newly imported from warm climates into temperate regions before putting them straight into the aviary. The best method of doing this is to keep them in a heated birdroom at the back of the aviary and gradually reduce the heat each day until it is safe for them to go into the aviary during the day, but be sure to lock them in again at night during any cold weather. Once acclimatized, you can keep finches outside until the autumn in most temperate climates. After that time, move them indoors and keep them at a temperature no lower than 10°C(50°F). Also cover part of the aviary roof to provide shelter from heavy rain.

Finches are very sociable birds and should not be kept alone. In fact, it is possible to keep quite a large number of finches together, ideally in pairs because they will live much longer that way. Being active birds, it is quite common for finches to quarrel among themselves, particularly so between newly established pairs. If you

Above: The grey singing finch is not the most colourful of species, but compensates for this by being a fine songster with a pleasant disposition and lively nature. It is a hardy bird that will mix well and sing for hours. This is an ideal choice for an outside aviary where you wish to mix different species.

Right: The green singing finch has a delightful song and will sing almost constantly. As this photograph suggests, it is a close relative of the canary. These birds can be mixed with other species in an aviary, but they will breed much better inside, where they can be kept in warmer and more stable conditions.

What exactly are finches in birdkeeping terms?

The true finches belong to the family Fringillidae, but when most people refer to finches they cover a large number of birds from other families, such as Estrildidae (waxbills, mannikins, munias and allies), Viduinae (viduine weavers and whydahs) and Ploceidae (weavers and sparrows). Which species belongs to which family is not a priority for beginners, but the needs of each species or group that have similar requirements is important. Therefore the weavers, mannikins and whydahs are separated in this book, not for scientific reasons but because they have different requirements and are commonly kept in captivity. Waxbills also have their own page even though they are kept in a similar way to true finches.

Below: The red-winged pytilia is a stunning bird, but not such a good songster. It has been bred in captivity once it has settled in an aviary, but it is inclined to be a bit scatty and mess around making various nests.

wish to have an aviary full of finches, make sure that you keep only one pair from each species; this will prevent aggressiveness and fighting. Providing an aviary spacious enough for the birds to keep out of each other's way will also prevent quarrels, as will offering plenty of perches and places to roost, plus at least two nestboxes or wicker baskets per pair.

A basic seed mixture suitable for finches consists of yellow millet, white millet, red millet, canary grass seed and a selection of smaller seeds, such as rape seed. All seedeaters should also have grit available to them so that they can digest the hard seeds once they have swallowed them. You should find that your birds will eat this diet readily, but livefood and greenfood prove to be healthy enticements. Checking that your birds are eating well by looking for an empty feeding dish is an unsound strategy; because the discarded husks of consumed seeds remain in the feeding dish, you are very unlikely to discover their feeding dish entirely empty. In fact, the husks can create a health hazard by covering up the uneaten seed beneath. As well as cleaning out and refilling the seed dishes regularly, also remove any remaining greenfood or livefood every day to prevent any health hazard developing.

It is also vital to provide a dish of fresh clean water every day, especially throughout the warm months. Small birds such as finches need to drink very often, and if the water supply ceases halfway through a hot day, you may discover several dead and dehydrated finches on the aviary floor in the evening.

Although not quite so melodious, some finches are considerably easier to keep than canaries or budgerigars and are therefore highly suitable for beginners. As with the majority of small birds, however, their lifespan is fairly short, usually about five to eight years.

A number of finches kept in a spacious aviary should breed very well, provided they are not overcrowded. Once you exceed the optimum number of finches in the aviary, i.e. when the birds are breeding and the youngsters remain in the aviary, you will notice that breeding become less productive and the lack of space causes many disputes to break out between the birds.

It can be very difficult, if not impossible, to sex some of the finches by observation; in many species, the male and female look identical. You should refer to detailed reference books covering the relevant species. A good plan is to buy about six birds of the same species, place split rings of different colours on their legs and then watch them sort themselves into pairs. Although this is not always an infallible method, you should be able to find at least one pair.

When finches enter the breeding season, you will discover that within a few days they will have already filled their nestboxes or wicker baskets with the appropriate material before they begin to lay their eggs. Providing finches with nesting containers and materials is

Above: The melba finch is best kept in single pairs, as the males are aggressive even outside the breeding season. House the finches in an inside area that has access to a well-planted aviary in the summer. Once acclimatized, they will breed quite easily among any dense bushes planted in the outside aviary.

easy. The wicker baskets or traditional small nestboxes, dried grass and coconut fibres are widely available from pet stores.

An average clutch ranges from three to six eggs and a pair can lay a whole clutch within four days. The majority of finch eggs are either white or cream in colour and are the most delicate of eggs, so handle them with extreme care. The incubation period can last for 12-15 days and once the chicks hatch, fledging occurs 14-28 days later, depending on the species. Very soon after fledging, the adults will begin to breed again. They are quite capable of raising two broods every year, usually one directly after the other. It is advisable to remove the chicks from the aviary at the end of the year to prevent overcrowding, since the chicks are quite capable of breeding the following year.

Left: *The star finch is one of the more delicate species of finch and will need more privacy than most other species. It can be bred in captivity in a well-planted aviary that is not disturbed too often, but be warned - once the birds start to nest leave them well alone, otherwise they will desert their nests.*

Below: *The diamond sparrow normally reaches a length of 11.5cm(4.5in), but is susceptible to becoming overweight in captivity. To avoid this, house the birds in an aviary where they can exercise, rather than in a cage, and also ration the amount of livefood you give them.*

63

Below: *The Bicheno finch is a favourite species among birdkeepers. Not only does it have unusual markings, it also has a delightful temperament, not unlike that of the Bengalese and zebra finches. Bichenos are perhaps not the first species you should buy if you wish to breed birds. You may find you have a pair that are good at laying eggs but fall far short of what is required when it comes to incubating and rearing their young. In such a case, Bengalese finches can be used as foster parents for Bicheno eggs. To breed birds successfully, first gain some experience with commoner species, such as the zebra finch.*

Left: The zebra finch is by far the most common finch species kept in captivity. It is easy to keep and has no special dietary requirements. This factor, together with a lovely disposition, makes zebra finches an ideal species for the beginner to birdkeeping. Once you have a pair of finches in good health and you add a nestbox to their enclosure, you won't be able to stop them breeding.

Right: Almost any collection of finches will be lacking something if the vivid colours of a pair of Gouldian finches are not included. Since these birds are natives of northern Australia, they appreciate a good deal of warmth and protection from cold and drizzly conditions. Gouldian finches are quiet and shy birds that prefer to be housed with their own kind. They can be bred if kept in fairly dry conditions.

Below: The red-faced parrot finch is not a bird that does well in a caged environment. It is best suited to an outside aviary furnished with planted edges or corners for privacy, but with open spaces for the birds to fly in, as they are agile finches that fly at speed. They do need warm conditions and you should not allow the temperature to drop below 19°C(66°F) for best results. If you can provide these conditions then you should have no problems in breeding them.

Left: *Fawn Bengalese finches, like all Bengalese finches, are unusual in that they are best housed and bred in cages. This is because they are highly sociable and like to crowd together in a nest, seeming not to worry about their eggs, which are often broken. Sometimes, all the females in a group will lay in the same nest and all try to incubate at the same time. Because of this, it is always better to keep the birds in pairs and to separate the young soon after fledging; otherwise, they will be still be in the nest when the next clutch is laid.*

Right: *A male and female pintailed nonpareil. They tend to become obese in cages and have a short lifespan, so keep them in an aviary with other finches, which encourages them to exercise. They are not easy to breed; keep them in temperatures above 16°C (just over 60°F), as they do not sleep in nests, and warmer during the breeding season.*

Left: The cut-throat finch is easy to keep in captivity, but bear in mind that given warm conditions to start with, the birds do best in an outside aviary. They normally mix well, but watch out for the rogue bully. Cut-throats can be bred but will sometimes leave a nest for no apparent reason.

Above: This beautiful golden song sparrow has a song not unlike the house sparrow. It is a fairly shy bird that needs its privacy in an outside aviary. You can mix it with other species, but do keep an eye on it, as it has been known to behave spitefully, especially close to the breeding season.

Below: The bold colours of the Java sparrow make it a popular bird. Furthermore, it is not fussy about its food or quarters. However, remember that this bird is 14cm(5.5in) long, so if it is kept inside, it will need a cage at least 120cm(48in) on a side. Java sparrows will live in a mixed aviary with no problems.

Waxbills

Waxbills are delicate birds when first imported and you must take care not to allow them to become chilled. Once acclimatized, the more common species have proved to be quite hardy in an aviary that is well protected from any strong draughts and has a good, dry, snug shelter.

During the winter, waxbills do need to feed for longer than the hours of daylight, so it is a good idea to have some sort of light on a time switch to extend the light for a few hours. To help keep the birds warm in the night shelter, build a small shelf 15cm(6in) below the roof where they can roost. If you keep several birds together, this will work very well indeed. You can also add some small branches from a shrub on this shelf, which will give them even more security. These delightful birds love splashing around in a shallow water dish, which should be provided as a permanent feature. In general, waxbills can be kept and bred in aviaries or cages without encountering any major problems.

For breeding, waxbills will require domed wicker nest baskets or nestboxes with half-open fronts. Several different types are available, but generally the nestbox needs to be covered. In a large aviary furnished with some dense shrubs or bushes, waxbills will build domed nests but they are often rather lazy about doing this. Waxbills' diet is basically the same as for other finches and they will take greenfood, such as chickweed and groundsel, but they are more insectivorous. Any plants in the aviary that flower and attract insects are always appreciated as these birds will welcome any livefood. Most species of finches need livefood in the breeding season, but this is even more important for waxbills, as they rear their chicks almost completely on livefood. Do not give them too many mealworms, however, as this is dangerous. Try to offer the birds as great a variety of livefood as possible, but keep it on the small side. If you have any plants that are covered in greenfly or blackfly and you can move them temporarily into the aviaries, the birds will greatly appreciate this addition to their diet.

Waxbills tend to have great affection for one another and this is why people tend to keep them in pairs, often housing several pairs in an aviary or cage. However, do not be tempted to overcrowd them; even though they are sociable, they never seem to do so well.

Charming birds from warm areas of the world

The waxbills belong to the family Estrildidae and are a group of small finches that live in the grasslands and forest edges in the tropical regions of Africa, with a few species from Asia and one from Australia. They are all attractive birds with a unique charm that is all their own. The name 'waxbill' is derived from their stout reddish beaks that look like sealing wax.

Below: A pair of red-billed firefinches. These gorgeous little birds are very susceptible to disease if recently imported and will need plenty of warmth. Keep them at temperatures of 19°C(66°F) or above. Other than this, they are easy to keep and suitable for the beginner. If you have provided somewhere for them to nest, they will try and breed soon after they have settled in.

Right: The red-cheeked cordon bleu is a beautiful bird and cordon bleus are among the most popular of all of the exotic finches kept in captivity. They may be popular but they are not easy to keep. When you first introduce them to a new aviary, be sure to watch them for a while until they know their way around. At night, they roost on a perch and not in a nestbox, so they require a warm area to roost in, say 19°C(66°F) or more. They can be kept in an aviary or cage, but only in pairs at breeding time, as males can be aggressive.

Weavers

Because of their spectacular nest-building activities, weavers are among the most interesting small birds to keep in captivity. They are extremely spirited birds that will spend their lifetimes collecting materials to create their unique nests. Each species builds its own individual style of nest, and some can be absolutely incredible. Watching them build their nests, intricate as they are, can be a truly relaxing experience. Not surprisingly, it is vital to keep these birds well supplied with nest-building material; if you fail to do so, they will automatically destroy each others' nests to fuel their own building activities. Although preferred nesting material varies slightly between species, most will avidly make use of long strands of semi-dried grass.

Although fairly small - about 12.5cm(5in) - weavers still require housing in a large, well-planted aviary; unlike other small seedeaters, they will only thrive in an outdoor environment and should not be housed indoors. Fortunately, weavers are hardy birds and so it is relatively easy to care for them during cold weather. You will need to lock them in at night once the winter approaches in temperate climates, but they are still among the toughest and also most active of all the finch-type birds.

Feeding weavers is very straightforward, for they will thrive on a basic finch seed mixture, plus a small amount of fruit and greenfood. It is also a good idea to offer baby mealworms or baby crickets as regular treats.

Weavers have a reputation for being rather aggressive, especially during the breeding season. In fact, some species are best housed on their own, one species to an aviary. If you mix unsuited species, the birds will destroy each others' nests and this will obviously lead to fighting. Weavers are most compatible with birds of a similar size.

Breeding weavers can be difficult and unsuccessful, and

Industrious nest-builders from Africa and Asia

Most of the weavers kept as captive birds are native to Africa, south of the Sahara, although some species are found in India and range into Southeast Asia. The familiar house sparrow belongs to one of the subfamilies of these Old World seedeaters. Many of the more colourful weavers have an eclipse plumage out of their breeding season - which varies according to their countries of origin. Out of the breeding season, the colourful males moult their splendid feathers and assume the drab brown colouring that the females have throughout the year. Weavers are social birds and if they are compatible many different species can be kept together without problems.

Below: The red-billed quelea has been imported in very large numbers. They are easy to keep and are always building nests, but they hardly ever breed in captivity.

Right: The stunning orange bishops are a pleasure to have in bird collection. They are always active and their brilliant colours guarantee a good display. As with many weavers, the orange bishops are busy nearly all the time with nest building, but are not often bred in captivity. They can be housed in cages, but after a few months they slowly lose their colour and become much paler.

Above: The chestnut, or chocolate, weaver does not have bright colours to match some of the dazzling birds in this group, but it is still very pleasing to the eye with its light chocolate colour plumage and bold black head. Once acclimatized to conditions in temperate climates, this is a hardy bird, but it is not kept in captivity in large numbers and has not proved easy to breed.

so they are not bred in captivity on a very large scale. Often you will find that after building one nest, they will not breed but simply begin to build another nest, and so on. Therefore, it is very important to give weavers some privacy; if they are continually disturbed, they will not breed at all. In some species, males and females have a different colouring, but in the majority the cock and hen birds look identical; scientific sexing is the only accurate way of telling them apart. If you are fortunate enough to possess a pair of breeding weavers, you will find that they lay a clutch of 2-5 eggs. The incubation period is about 12-14 days, and fledging occurs 14 days later. It is a good idea to house a single cock with several hens; this not only encourages successful breeding, but also prevents aggressive behaviour between cock birds.

Whydahs

Whydahs are ideal subjects for housing with weavers or birds of a similar size. Because whydahs are among the largest and more aggressive species of finches, do not house them with birds of smaller or weaker species, such as smaller waxbills. Keep them in a large well-planted aviary, since they must have adequate room to exercise their active nature. Once acclimatized, they will be hardy enough to withstand typical winter conditions in a temperate climate, providing they have access to a snug and protective shelter. During nights of very severe winter weather, however, you should lock your birds in to protect them.

Feeding whydahs is relatively easy, because all they require is a simple mixture of yellow millet, white millet, canary grass seed and rape seed, although an excellent supplemental seed diet can consist of teazle, sunflower seed, flax, niger seed, anise, sesame seed, oats and poppy seed. They will also appreciate a selection of livefood, such as small mealworms and baby crickets, and a limited amount of suitable greenfood.

In addition to the simplicity of feeding and accommodating them, the great appeal of keeping whydahs centres around the magnificent appearance of cock birds throughout the breeding season and their fascinating courtship behaviour. The cock whydahs grow magnificent tail plumes that can reach 28-40cm(11-16in) long. Out of breeding season, whydahs measure only 13cm(5in) and cocks and hens appear very similar, making sexing a difficult task.

Many whydahs are parasitic and will lay their eggs in the nests of other birds. This is why it is vital to choose carefully which birds to house with your whydahs. Most parasitic whydahs target particular species. For example, the paradise whydah parasitizes the melba

Splendidly attired birds of the African continent

Whydahs are close relatives of the weavers and are found in the same areas of eastern and southern Africa, as well as in West and Central Africa. They have long been popular as cage and aviary birds because of their long and varied tails.

Right: A male queen whydah in breeding plumage. This magnificent bird is very popular for showing. You can keep several males together, but not with females. Otherwise, the birds are best kept in pairs to avoid fighting.

Inset right: The drably coloured female queen whydah seems rather small compared to its beautiful partner. The female is about 13cm(5in) long, whereas the male bird in breeding plumage can measure 25-33cm(10-13in) in length.

Above: A male pintailed whydah in breeding plumage; the tail feathers look completely out of proportion! It is a hardy bird and can be kept in an outside aviary, but as it is very spiteful, do not mix it with similarly sized birds.

finch in the wild and will also accept it as a host in captivity. Therefore, if you wish to breed paradise whydahs, it is essential to house it with melba finches. The pintail whydah parasitizes more than one species; in fact, it can lay its eggs in the nests of 19 different species of birds.

Although fascinating, their parasitic behaviour produces a poor breeding record in captivity. Nevertheless, you can encourage breeding by housing the birds in a large, naturally planted aviary with a plentiful supply of available nests. Providing the ideal environment is essential for breeding success.

On average, whydah clutches consist of 3-4 eggs. These are incubated for 14 days and the young leave the nest after a further 14 days. Do not be too disappointed if your birds fail to breed, because they can be particularly difficult. Do bear in mind that whydahs are principally kept as display birds and not for breeding purposes. Because of their amazing plumages, whydahs are often used for bird shows as well as forming the centrepiece in many birdkeepers' gardens.

Above: The paradise whydah is a very popular aviary bird and the most striking of all the commonly kept foreign birds. This is a hardy, easy to keep bird that will not bother other birds or destroy any plants in the aviary.

Mannikins

These birds are a convenient size for keeping in captivity, varying from 9.5 to 12.5cm(3.75-5in), and are best housed in a well-planted aviary. Not only are mannikins attractive to look at, but they are also extremely active and therefore fun to watch. Do not mistake their general liveliness as aggression when they chase each other around the aviary, although some do become aggressive in the breeding season and should be watched. Although they are active birds, they do need peaceful conditions in the aviary, especially if you wish to breed them. If you wish to keep a mannikin in an indoor cage or mixed aviary, choose a silverbill (a type of mannikin), as these are more suited to indoor and sociable situations.

Mannikins are relatively hardy to low temperatures, but must be protected from frost. If frost is forecast, be sure to bring your birds into a frost-free area and do not return them outside until you can be sure that the temperature will not drop below freezing again.

Mannikins are not fussy eaters, but they do appreciate a varied diet. This can consist of a universal seed mixture, plus greens, weed seeds and cuttlefish bone, especially in the breeding season.

A common health problem that frequently arises with mannikins is the rapid growth of their nails. This problem is particularly serious with a group of mannikins known as nuns, which will need their nails trimmed regularly. Mannikins do like to bathe, so make fresh, easily accessible bathing water available every day.

Differentiating the sexes is simply a matter of observing the behaviour of the birds, for it is the male that dances and sings. Unfortunately, some of the mannikins are inept at breeding in captivity; silverbills are among the more ready breeders.

Robust birds found widely in the Old World

Mannikins are found in Africa south of the Sahara Desert, Madagascar, India, Southeast Asia and Australia. They are all chunky birds with stout beaks for shelling seeds.

Left: As is clear from this photograph, the tricoloured nun is an aptly named bird. It is widely kept, not just because it is pleasing to the eye, but because it is very hardy in captivity. It can be kept safely outside during the winter months, as long as it has a snug and draught-free shelter. The tricoloured nun has been successfully bred in captivity but not in very large numbers.

Below: The spice finch is one of the most commonly imported Indian birds and found in almost every collection of finches. It mixes easily as long as the aviary is not overcrowded. It is hardly ever bred, but has crossed with several other species, so be careful when mixing them.

If you are intent on breeding mannikins, remove them from a mixed enclosure and place them in a small separate aviary. You will also need to provide plenty of dried grass and similar bedding material for the birds to use in constructing their nests.

Mannikins prefer to build their nests in shrubs and bushes, so a well-planted aviary is clearly a good idea. If this presents any problems, do not despair, for they will also accept traditional nestboxes. A good way of encouraging birds to breed is to provide plenty of livefood before the start of the breeding season. They are more likely to breed if they believe there will be an ample supply of livefood to feed to their growing youngsters. An average mannikin clutch consists of 3-6 eggs. These should hatch within 12-13 days and fledging should occur 14-30 days later, depending on the species.

Right: The attractive white-headed nuns have a friendly nature and can be easily mixed with other species without problems. However, you will need a great deal of experience to breed them, and even then there can be no guarantee of success. The white-headed nun is recommended as a good bird for the beginner to include in a mixed collection.

Left: The pretty pictorella finch is a fairly hardy bird, but watch out for it in sudden cold spells. It is not difficult to keep, in fact it is very easy, but breeding this species is relatively difficult. The pair may build a bulky nest of grass near the ground, but you often find that they never show any interest in nesting at all unless the aviary is big enough.

Below: The African silverbill is an excellent bird for the beginner. It is easy to keep, fairly hardy, and not fussy about its food. Furthermore, when it comes to breeding time, the birds will present you with no problems. The Indian silverbill requires exactly same care as its African counterpart.

Above: The pearl-headed silverbill, with its grey-and-white spotted head, will stand out in any mixed collection of birds. These social birds will breed readily once they have become fully acclimatized to temperate conditions.

Cardinals and buntings

Cardinals

At 16.5-23cm(6.5-9in), cardinals are the largest and strongest of the finch-type birds commonly kept in captivity. House these birds in a large, well-planted aviary. They are relatively hardy, and so do not require additional heat during the winter months, providing they have access to a cosy shelter. If housed with other birds, keep cardinals with the larger seedeaters; their most suitable companions are weavers, whydahs and Java sparrows. The yellow-billed cardinal is an excellent choice for a mixed aviary, for not only has it a placid nature, but it will also breed in captivity.

Cardinals are easy to feed. Their omnivorous diet consists of a simple seed mixture, fruit and insects, and they relish soaked wheat, oats and barley. Increase the quantities of these foods considerably - particularly the insects - throughout the breeding season.

When it comes to breeding cardinals, it is best to breed them in separate pairs rather than within a mixed group. At the onset of the breeding season, they can become surprisingly aggressive. The ease of distinguishing the sexes varies according to the species. Pope cardinals, for example, can be difficult to breed simply because the sexes are so similar and it is difficult to isolate a true pair. However, once you have a true pair of cardinals, there are various ways of encouraging them to breed. You can fix up an old blackbird's or thrush's nest in an isolated bush, for example. Also provide bushes in the aviary, but consider very carefully where you plant them. If the shrubs are too close to the front or side of the aviary, or if there is a path close by, the resultant disturbance may prevent them nesting altogether or cause them to abandon the nestsite halfway through the incubation period. The best idea is to plant dense shrubs at the back of the aviary in an area where any nesting birds are least likely to be disturbed.

Cardinals are quite capable of producing two or three broods each season, each clutch consisting of 2-3 eggs. Incubation takes about 13 days and the young chicks should leave the nest within the following two weeks. It is very important to remove the chicks at the earliest opportunity. If the adults decide to nest again while the chicks are still in the aviary, they may turn on their chicks and can kill them within a few hours. Be sure to monitor the behaviour of your birds during the breeding season to forestall such disasters. Also check the growing chicks for leg deformities, which cardinals are prone to developing. Adding a multivitamin supplement to the food or water should prevent these problems arising. If in doubt, ask your veterinarian for advice.

Sturdy woodland birds from the New World

Cardinals are part of the large family of New World seedeaters. They are native to tropical America, although some species range northwards into the United States and Canada, and south into Argentina.

Above: The red-crested cardinal is a truly stunning bird, with its red crest and face. Although it is a beautiful bird, it is not much of a songster. As long as you provide plenty of bushes in the aviary to give it a choice of nestsites, you should be able to achieve breeding success with this bird.

Right: The soft red colour of the male Virginian cardinal accounts for its popularity; hens are brown. It has a fairly good temperament and can be mixed with other birds of the same size or larger. If it has nesting bushes and a large amount of livefood at breeding time, you should have no problems.

Buntings

Buntings vary in size from 12 to 20cm(4.75-8in), depending on the species. Most are not suitable for being caged indoors, as this type of lifestyle causes them to become overweight. The rainbow and lazuli buntings, however, are not hardy and must therefore be housed indoors as soon as the cold weather approaches, but they must have sufficient room to exercise. An outside aviary for buntings should be as large as possible and situated in a warm sunny area. Some species can be kept outside all year round, providing they have easy access to a frost-proof shelter.

The standard diet for buntings is based on a seed mixture consisting of canary seed, millet oats, hemp and grass seeds, with additions of grated carrot, chopped chickweed and insects. When the breeding season arrives, it is essential to provide a lavish supply of insects, as they rear their young exclusively on them.

Most buntings are shy and retiring, so they make good mixers, although their considerable size may scare smaller species. Do not house the nonpareil, or painted bunting, with close relatives, however, as aggressive behaviour and fighting are likely to occur. Unfortunately, buntings are not bred in large numbers in captivity, as their breeding success is rather poor. When they do breed, they build cup-shaped nests in dense bushes or, alternatively, they will use half open nestboxes to lay their clutch of 4-6 eggs. The incubation period lasts approximately 12 days and fledging occurs 14 days later.

Above: The attractive rainbow bunting can be kept in a cage or aviary. These birds have a pleasant nature and are fairly easy to keep. It is best to house them inside in winter, but they do not require much heat.

Below: The extremely pretty golden-breasted bunting has a pleasant song and does well in a mixed collection. Keep it in an aviary, as it tends to get too fat in a cage.

Widespread and attractive

Buntings are found in both the New and the Old World. The American buntings belong to the same subfamily as the cardinals and are found from the United States to Panama. The Eurasian buntings belong to the genus *Emberiza* and range across the region into Japan as well as southwards into Africa.

Doves

Doves vary dramatically in size, the larger ones being referred to as pigeons. Doves are easy to accommodate, either indoors or outdoors, although pigeons are more suited to an outdoor environment. Fortunately, there are many varieties of domesticated doves that are hardy enough to be kept outdoors all year round, even in quite severe weather conditions. Exotic doves from very warm climates, however, will need housing in tropical conditions. If well cared for, doves can live for 10-14 years. Feeding doves is fairly simple, since they will readily accept seeds, berries, fruit and insects.

It is possible to keep doves with many other species of birds in an outdoor aviary and experience very little if any problems. However, it is not advisable to keep many doves together, because they appear to be intolerant of their own species and the males are likely to fight.

Part of the appeal of keeping doves is their tame nature. They can become surprisingly affectionate towards their owner, often to the point of ignoring other members of the family. One unfortunate

Below: The barbary dove is the commonest of the seven species of ring-necked doves, and now available in various colours. It is cheap to buy and easy to keep. Barbary doves are also very easy to breed and are often used as foster parents for more difficult species. Highly recommended for the beginner.

disadvantage of keeping doves is the abundance of their droppings. They produce a truly excessive amount of waste for their body size, which not only makes the cage or enclosure unhygienic, but is also aesthetically distasteful.

Once you have a pair settled in an aviary, many doves and pigeons can be quite free breeding. An average dove clutch consists of one or two eggs, very rarely will it exceed this. The hen and the cock share the responsibilities of incubating the eggs, which should last 14-19 days, depending on the species. Fledging occurs about 12-18 days later. Common and domesticated doves can produce up to three clutches per season, although the more exotic types usually produce only one.

Left: The laughing dove is a quiet and pleasant bird to keep. Like most doves, it is an excellent addition to a mixed collection of birds. This species is easy to breed and you can keep it outside all year round, as long you provide the security of a sheltered aviary with some good bushes to ensure its privacy.

Below: The diamond dove is widely kept and many people feel it is the best-looking of all the doves. It is extremely easy to keep and breed and is produced in very large numbers and in different colour forms. Its small size makes it popular, because it can be housed in a compact space. Diamond doves are often mixed with finches.

Familiar birds in all regions of the world

Pigeons and doves belong to the Columbidae family of birds and are found in all temperate and tropical regions of the world. There are over 280 species and are most varied in colour and form in the Australasian and oriental part of their range.

Quails

Quails are extremely adaptable ground birds with gentle, affectionate natures, and will live happily in both indoor and outdoor enclosures. They are also particularly suitable for mixing with various perching birds. Many people keep quails in an aviary, where they clear up seeds dropped by the other birds and consume any insects they happen to encounter.

As with many other birds, quails like to be kept dry and must be protected from draughts, so be sure to shelter them from the wind as much as possible. In cold temperate climates, make sure they have access to a bird house at night during the winter months.

Quails will thrive on a diet of mixed small seeds with a little added livefood. In fact, quails are not very fussy creatures and will consume practically anything you offer them.

Once they become familiar with their surroundings, quails settle down to become friendly, sociable birds, if a little nervous at times. In fact, be careful not to disturb quails suddenly, because they fly vertically into the air when startled and are likely to break their necks if they hit the wire of the enclosure. To prevent this happening with new birds clip one of the wings to temporarily inhibit their flight. When landscaping an enclosure to include quails, take into account that they have a habit of patrolling the perimeter fence and destroying any plants in their way.

Although quails are gregarious birds, it is not advisable to keep more than one pair in the same enclosure, as the males are likely to fight. Cocks in adjacent aviaries will try to attack each other through the mesh, so border the bottom 25cm(10in) of the aviaries with solid wood to keep the antagonists from seeing each other.

Quails are very easy to breed and will lay eggs prolifically. An average clutch consists of 4-12 eggs, although 16 or more is not uncommon. The incubation period lasts about 17 days. However, it is rare for captive quails to incubate the eggs and rear their youngsters. Since their eggs have usually been taken away and reared in incubators to maximize the yield from one pair of birds, quails have become inept at raising their own chicks.

Family members with partridges and pheasants

Quails are part of a large family of birds that includes partridges and pheasants. They are found in North, Central and South America, as well as across southern Asia and into Australia. At 18-28cm(7-11in), the American species are larger than those from Africa and Asia, which reach 14-18cm(5.5-7in).

Above: The Japanese quail is an excellent bird for beginners. It is easy to keep and will thrive in an aviary that measures just 1.5m(4ft) on a side. Since there are many hybrids available, it can be difficult to buy a true form.

Right: *The Chinese painted quail is also easy to keep and will live and breed in an area 1m(39in) square. Thousands are bred every year in captivity. Watch over the young; they are so small that they can escape through 1.25cm(0.5in) mesh.*

Below: *Although it can be kept in area of 1.5m(4ft) square, the scaled quail prefers a larger space. It is commonly kept by experienced birdkeepers but is not really suitable for beginners.*

Cockatiels

Cockatiels reach a size of about 32cm(12.5in) and will normally live for 10-14 years, although some birds have reached the age of 30. These are relatively hardy birds that you can keep indoors or outdoors, as long as you provide a suitable shelter in an outdoor environment. Cockatiels thrive on exercise and so need a spacious rectangular cage or aviary. You should also provide them with a suitable bathing dish, and be sure to change the water every day.

Feeding cockatiels is similar to parakeets; a good-quality budgie mix supplemented with milo (a round red seed also known as red dari), sunflower seed and safflower seed will suit them fine. Daily supplies of fruit and vegetables, together with ground white oyster shell or cuttlefish, are also essential for good health.

With their ease of taming and attractively mischievous nature, it is not surprising that cockatiels have become exceedingly popular as pet birds throughout the world. Not only are they capable of talking and whistling, but they can also perform tricks.

Cockatiels are ideal for housing with budgerigars. Birds about the same size as cockatiels are also compatible, but do not mix them with large parrots, as they will undoubtedly fall victim to attack, and from a large parrot this could mean serious injury to the cockatiel or even death.

It is possible to pick out cock birds within a group of young cockatiels because they tend to have brighter, more striking facial markings and larger crests. It is also possible to recognize adult hens because the majority retain the distinctive barring on the underside of the tail. To be absolutely sure, it is best to have the birds scientifically sexed.

Cockatiels are unlikely to breed before they are 18 months old. When they do enter the breeding season, they need a large cage and a large nestbox. Two clutches are produced a year on average, each consisting of 4-8 white eggs. These are incubated for 18-20 days, and the young fledge 35 days after hatching. Privacy is essential for breeding to be successful.

Below: A pair of grey cockatiels. The form pictured here is the one most commonly kept in captivity. The difference between the male and female is clear to see: the male's face is much yellower and bolder than the female's.

Common and noisy birds of the Australian interior

Cockatiels are small parrots native to Australia, where they are extremely common in the interior rather than around the coastal regions. They fly swiftly, sometimes in large flocks, and feed mainly on seeds and fruits.

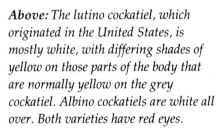

Above: *The lutino cockatiel, which originated in the United States, is mostly white, with differing shades of yellow on those parts of the body that are normally yellow on the grey cockatiel. Albino cockatiels are white all over. Both varieties have red eyes.*

Right: *The cinnamon pearl (r) and pied cockatiels are two popular varieties that are widely kept and bred. The fact that breeders are able to produce cockatiels in such a variety of subtle colours and markings is one reason for the increasing popularity of these birds.*

Parakeets

Parakeets vary in size quite dramatically, ranging from 14 to 40cm (12-16in), and the choice of species is equally wide. Housing parakeets should present no major problems - the majority of species will thrive outdoors in the fresh air, although you must make sure that the aviary provides ample room for flight and exercise and a sturdy shelter to protect the birds from frost, wind and rain. It is also a good idea to cover a third of the aviary roof with plastic sheeting or similar material, as this enables the birds to shelter from any bad weather conditions but still remain outdoors. Almost all species of parakeets will survive typical winter conditions in a temperate climate, although you should lock them in at night during particularly severe conditions.

As for all parrots, an aviary housing parakeets must be able to withstand the attentions of their powerful beaks. If the aviary is made of wood, for example, it is vital to protect the exposed areas so that they are not destroyed. Even though you may not consider your birds to have powerful beaks because they are relatively small, they are very capable of gnawing the same area for a long period of time and causing extensive damage. This is why you should supply your parakeets with plenty of chewing materials, such as wooden perches, and replace these every two months.

A suitable diet for parakeets varies slightly according to the birds' size. The basic diet for a small parakeet, for example, should consist of mixed millet, canary seed, hemp and sunflower seeds, with additional fruit and vegetables. Larger species will need more sunflower seeds and perhaps some small peanuts and pine nuts.

One advantage of keeping parakeets rather than the larger parrot species is that they make considerably less noise. Obviously they do still chatter, but this can prove to be pleasant rather than annoying. However, it is not necessarily a good idea to locate the aviary too close to your house, as they pick up the habit of chattering rather too early in the morning! Although it is possible to house some of the smaller parakeets in a mixed aviary, where they will happily live with even smaller birds, such as finches, they are happier housed on their own and this will also enhance their breeding prospects.

Sexing parakeets is not the easiest of tasks, for although some species have visible external differences, the majority need scientific sexing. Do not be fooled into thinking that just because a pair of

Right: A male ringneck parakeet - one of the most common parakeets to be bred in captivity on a regular basis. They are not too noisy and always available at relatively low cost. If you are thinking of acquiring a pair of parakeets, this species is a good one to start with.

birds get on very well, they must consist of a cock and hen; often, two males or two females will behave like a 'pair'. If you have any doubts, have the birds scientifically sexed.

Once the breeding season approaches, you must choose the correct size of nestbox for your particular species. It is difficult to generalize because of the extensive size range among parakeets. The majority of parakeet species will breed readily, producing one or perhaps two clutches a year. The clutch size, incubation period and time of fledging varies depending on body size. The smaller species, for example, lay between two and seven eggs, the incubation period lasts 18-21 days and fledging will most likely occur 42-45 days later. The larger parakeets yield an average clutch of two to four eggs, which are incubated for 21-28 days and the young fledge 42-56 days later. At the end of the breeding season, it is always advisable to remove the nestboxes, as some parakeets will attempt to breed during the winter months and this is likely to lead to egg-binding. It is very important, therefore, to supply a nestbox only when signs of bad weather have disappeared.

Below: The bright, multicoloured golden mantled parakeet is large but very easy to keep. The female has less red than the male (shown here) but is still multicoloured. Once you have a compatible pair, they will breed for many years without problems.

Below: Bourke's grass parakeets are widely kept in captivity due to their quiet and also very friendly nature. This, together with the fact that they are easy to keep and do not require a large enclosure, means that they are well-suited to birdkeepers who do not have much room. Neighbours should not be disturbed by their call, as most of the time this is a pleasing whistle that only changes to a slightly louder call when the birds are in flight. They are inexpensive to buy, mainly because once you have a good pair, breeding them is very easy indeed. The grass parakeet shown here is a Rosa mutation and several more mutations have appeared in recent years.

Parrots with long tails

The term 'parakeet' is used to describe members of the parrot family with long tails. Parakeets of various species are found in tropical and subtropical regions across the world, including Central and South America, Africa, India, southern Asia and Australia (including Tasmania).

Below: The delightful plumhead parakeet has a pleasing nature and is a favourite with birdkeepers. As you can see in this photograph, the male has a magnificent deep red and purple head, while the female is easily recognized by her dull bluish grey head and a variable yellow collar rather than a black one.

Below: *Quaker parakeets may not be the most striking of all the parakeets, but are probably the most interesting because of the way they breed. They require no nestboxes, just branches of hawthorn bushes. They will continually chew off material from the branches and use this to build nests measuring up to 1m(39in) or more across. You can keep these birds on a colony basis, which means that you will have several pairs breeding in one large twig ball.*

Above: *This stunning crimson-winged parakeet is one of the largest parakeets you will come across, growing up to 33cm(13in). It is shyer by nature than other parakeets but, unfortunately, just as destructive. In a spacious aviary, the male birds, with their large red wing patches, provide a spectacular display as they fly around the enclosure. However, females are less brightly coloured.*

Lovebirds

Lovebirds range in size from 13 to 15cm (4.5-6in), and for such comparatively small birds, they do have a relatively long lifespan of 10-15 years. As members of the parrot family, they are intelligent and have an inquisitive personality.

Housing lovebirds presents no problems, for a typical aviary used for accommodating parakeets is more than suitable, providing they have easy access to an inside enclosure and that a third of the roof is covered with plastic sheeting to offer shelter from heavy rain. It is possible to keep lovebirds in relatively small cages, although the minimum size should be 90x60x60cm(3x2x2ft); anything smaller is not acceptable. Once acclimatized, most lovebirds are hardy birds and will live very happily in an outdoor environment. More delicate species, such as the Madagascar, or grey-headed, lovebird, however, will be happier if accommodated inside.

The disadvantage of keeping lovebirds is that they can be particularly aggressive with any species other than their own. Never house lovebirds in a mixed aviary. It is possible to keep them on a colony basis, but this requires some experience and cannot be recommended to beginners. At the outset, it would be advisable to keep lovebirds in pairs.

It is vital to provide and regularly renew supplies of chewing material, as lovebirds adore to chew. Also try to create an interesting environment for the birds; if they become bored they may seek amusement in plucking each other's feathers.

As with housing, feeding lovebirds should present little complications. They will thrive on a simple seed mixture consisting of canary seed, millet, rape seed, sesame seed and oats, supplemented with milo (small round seeds also known as red dari), sunflower seed, safflower seed and greenfood, although, as with all parrot species, cuttlefish bone is often welcome.

There are no external differences between the sexes in most lovebirds, so they must be scientifically sexed. (The exceptions are the Abyssinian and Madagascar lovebirds, in which the females are basically green but the males have coloured heads.) The breeding behaviour of this group is known to be rather unusual, for not only do they build their nests within the actual nesting chamber, but many species also transport the nesting material

Below: The friendly and very appealing peach-faced lovebird is the most common and easily available of all lovebirds. These little birds are not very noisy and can be kept close to the house without causing too many problems. Being easy to keep and breed, the peach-faced lovebird is ideal for newcomers to the birdkeeping hobby.

Below: With their distinctive red beaks and black heads, the masked lovebirds are easy to recognize. They also have a fleshy white circle around each eye and belong to the 'white eye-ring' group. Although they have become more available in recent years, they are still relatively expensive and are usually kept by more experienced birdkeepers.

Short-tailed parrots from Africa and nearby islands

There are nine species of lovebirds and all are found in Africa, some of them in quite localized areas.

Above: The Fischer's lovebird is widely kept and, like all lovebirds, has a friendly nature. These birds are often kept on a colony basis *with other species of lovebirds. They are very active during the breeding season and are a particular pleasure to watch during this period of the year.*

in a very bizarre way - by carrying it in the plumage of the rump rather than in the beak. They like to strip bark from branches for nesting - especially willow - so provide a supply of fresh branches.

Lovebirds are quite capable of interbreeding with other species, and this is another good reason why they should only be housed with their own species. The peach-faced and Fischer's lovebird will breed readily if kept in pairs with sufficient nesting materials. Rarer species tend to be more difficult to breed, but with experience you should succeed. An average lovebird clutch consists of three to seven whitish eggs, usually laid twice a year. The incubation period is 18-24 days and fledging should occur 42-56 days later.

Conures

With a size range of 16-45cm(6.3-18in), conures can be classed as medium-sized parrots and, if well cared for, they will live up to 20 years or more in captivity.

The most suitable housing conditions for these birds are within a large outside aviary. Compared to parakeets, conures are excessively noisy birds and most are too large to be kept in an indoor cage as pets. The cactus conure is an exception and is more suited to a spacious indoor cage. As with most parrots, conures can cope with the majority of winter climates once they are acclimatized, providing they have adequate shelter. Only in extreme conditions will you need to lock them in.

A good conure diet should consist mainly of larger seeds, such as sunflower, safflower, and peanuts, plus some millet. You should have no problems buying typical parrot mixes suitable for your size of bird. Remember to offer supplements of fruit and greenfood.

Conures are much cheaper to maintain in good health than larger parrots, but they do produce excessive amounts of noise. Some species are worse than others, but in general, all conures are vociferous. They are also extremely destructive birds, so you will need to replace the perches in the enclosure every four weeks or so.

Slender-bodied parrots from the New World

Over 50 species and subspecies of conures are found in the New World, from southern Mexico to South America. They have slender bodies and relatively long tails, but not as long as those of parakeets compared to their body size.

Left: The peach-fronted conure is one of the smallest conures and does not have the boldness associated with the larger species. If you would like to breed these birds successfully, be sure to give them more privacy during the breeding season.

Left: The energetic red-fronted conure is a pleasure to keep, provided that you can cope with a bird that never seems to rest and a noise that, while not exactly deafening, never seems to stop. Be sure to give the birds plenty of wood to destroy to work off their endless energy.

Right: Nanday conures are ideal for beginners, because they are hardy birds and easy to keep. Like all conures, they are noisy, but once you have established a compatible pair, you will be able to breed them for many years.

To help prevent rapid destruction, cover the connection between the perch and the aviary with sheet metal or strong wire mesh. Otherwise, you will discover that within a week the bird has chewed the edge of the perch and it will have fallen to the floor. Do not replace wooden perches with plastic or metal ones, however, because it is essential for the birds to chew if they are to remain healthy and happy.

Some conures can be kept on a colony basis, but this requires more attention and cost than keeping them as pairs. Sexing conures is not the easiest of tasks; the majority of species have no external differences and so it is best to have them scientifically sexed to ensure that you have a true pair. Many species of conures can be successfully bred in captivity. The clutch varies from two to five eggs, sometimes seven, depending on the species. The incubation period lasts 23-28 days and the young fledge approximately 56 days later. When supplying the nestbox, add an inner lining of wood chips and bark to prevent the birds destroying the nestbox itself. Conures will not tolerate interference within the nestbox, and so for successful breeding leave the birds totally undisturbed during this period.

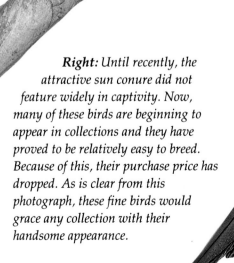

Right: Until recently, the attractive sun conure did not feature widely in captivity. Now, many of these birds are beginning to appear in collections and they have proved to be relatively easy to breed. Because of this, their purchase price has dropped. As is clear from this photograph, these fine birds would grace any collection with their handsome appearance.

Macaws

Many people keep macaws as pets; some species live up to 60 years or more and can therefore provide a lifetime of companionship. Their considerable size of 30-100cm(12-39in) means that macaws demand a great deal of time, attention and space. They can either be housed in a spacious outside aviary, which will need to be substantially built from highly durable materials, or alternatively, they can be kept outside in a large barrel 'home' with various perches in the surrounding area. Birds kept in this manner must have one winged clipped, however, to stop them flying away.

Once acclimatized, macaws can become particularly hardy birds that can remain outdoors all year round, except during severe winter conditions, when they should be locked in at night. It is essential to supply chewing material, not only to save unintended materials from destruction, but also to keep the bird healthy and contented. The blue and gold macaw is commonly kept as a caged pet due to its placid temperament, but other familiar species, such as the scarlet macaw, are not really suitable for this arrangement.

Feeding macaws is as simple as feeding other parrots. They love all the large seeds and nuts, such as sunflower seeds, peanuts, pine nuts, and will readily accept plenty of fruit and vegetables. Do remember that nuts are a fattening food and ration the amount you provide according to your bird's housing arrangements. A bird kept in a large flight or aviary, for example, can burn off any extra calories through exercise and so can be offered a larger number of nuts than one kept in an indoor cage. It is very important to monitor the diet and weight gain of your bird on a regular basis, particularly if you keep it indoors as a pet, because pet birds are especially susceptible to becoming unhealthily overweight in this way. Macaws are exceptionally

Right: The scarlet macaw is widely kept in captivity because of its magnificent colour. Over the last few years it has been bred in larger numbers, which is fortunate because the wild populations of these birds are steadily decreasing. Unfortunately, compared to other macaws in captivity, the scarlet macaw can have an objectionable nature.

Above: Green-winged macaws, among the largest species, are inquisitive by ature. Their large size and their massive and powerful beaks means that you must protect any wood, thin wire or loose brickwork that you do not want them to destroy with pleasure.

intelligent birds and will remember any mistreatment and recognize the culprit. Compared to a human being, macaws have a mental age of a four year-old child, and so you must treat them as such. You cannot leave them in a cage in a corner of a room over a long period of time, for example, as this will cause them long-term damage. As well as being noisy, macaws can also be particularly vicious and dangerous. They can sever a human finger, for example, with their extremely powerful beaks. Therefore, treat macaws with the utmost respect. You can keep macaws on their own or in pairs. However, do not make the mistake of feeling sorry for a tame solitary bird by purchasing a mate, as it will never be tame again.

Sexing macaws can prove difficult, as there are few external differences between the sexes. Within some species, the cocks may have bigger and bolder heads, but this is not a particularly accurate method of sexing them. With expensive birds such as macaws, it is always best to have them sexed scientifically. Macaws have bred successfully in captivity, although rarely before the birds are four years old. An average clutch consists of two or three white eggs, the incubation period lasts 25-28 days and the young fledge 8-15 weeks later.

Magnificent macaws from Mexico to South America

The 30 species and subspecies of these magnificent parrots live in the tropical forests of Central and South America. Unfortunately, much of the lowland forest of South America in which these lively and colourful birds live is disappearing fast.

Right: Blue and gold macaws have beaks just as powerful and potentially destructive as other macaws, as shown here by the ease with which these birds can open even the toughest nuts. But blue and gold macaws have a much more friendly nature than other species and because of this, they are the most commonly kept macaws in captivity.

97

Cockatoos

Being rather large parrots, approximately 30-67cm(12-27in), cockatoos do have a relatively long lifespan of 25-45 years, although some have lived considerably longer. The substantial size and strength of these birds does not make it easy to control their destructive and vociferous nature. If housed outside, they need a well-built, resilient aviary with mesh that will withstand constant attention from their powerful beaks. Perches will be rapidly destroyed and will need replacing about every two weeks. Cockatoos become hardy once acclimatized and will only need locking in when temperatures fall below freezing point.

Cockatoos are commonly kept as pets, the smaller species being more appropriate because of their less boisterous nature. All cockatoos are intelligent and should be treated as such. The larger species really are excessively noisy and you must take this into account when siting their aviary. Make sure it is not too close to your house, or your neighbour's for that matter!

A cockatoo diet is very similar to that for macaws - a good parrot mix of large seeds and nuts, such as sunflower seeds, pine nuts and peanuts, with additional fruit and vegetables. It is important not to curb a cockatoo's destructive inclinations, for this is natural and instinctive behaviour. The best policy is to provide plenty of suitable materials; if you do not, the bird will simply chew up any material available, and this can prove harmful. Cockatoos produce an excessive amount of feather dust, and are therefore unsuitable for anyone with asthma or any other lung-related disorders.

You can keep cockatoos singly or in pairs. There are few external differences between the cock and hen birds. Males tend to be slightly larger than females and have completely black irises compared to the reddish brown

Distinctive crested parrots from the South Pacific

There are about 20 species of cockatoos distributed across Australia, the Philippines, New Guinea and the nearby islands in the South Pacific. Those most often seen in captivity belong to the genus *Cacatua*.

Right: The all-white umbrella cockatoo is a large and often bold bird. As you can see, the bird in this picture has raised its crest, which it does when alarmed or interested in something. Note also the bird's powerful and destructive beak; if the bird is not tame, be sure to keep away from it. Another point to remember is that these are extremely noisy birds.

Left: The citron-crested cockatoo is one of the smaller species, with a splendid orange crest. Although they are still destructive by nature, these birds tend to be more friendly and quieter compared to the larger species of cockatoos. This is a subspecies of the lesser sulphur-crested cockatoo and is found only on the island of Sumba in Indonesia.

Below: The unusual roseate cockatoo, a native of Australia, is a shy bird compared to the normally bold cockatoos and therefore relatively quiet. It is much sought after by birdkeepers due to its stunning colours, compared to most other cockatoos. Unfortunately, the price of these birds is always high, but they have become increasingly available in recent years as they have been bred in greater numbers. Keep them individually or in pairs.

tinge in females, but this is a rather unreliable method of sexing. It is much better to have your birds scientifically sexed.

Cockatoos are often bred successfully in captivity. When breeding cockatoos, it is essential to use a nestbox of the correct size for the size of the bird. You may find it necessary to line the nestbox with sheet metal or wire mesh. This is because cockatoos do not stop chewing, even when they are breeding. In some cases, they dismantle the nestbox to such an extent that they are discouraged from rearing their young. Wire mesh or sheet metal will prevent them from destroying the nestbox, but offering additional chunks of wood will help to divert their attention.

Cockatoos are particularly private birds, especially during the breeding season. The Moluccan cockatoo is a good example of this; to rear their youngsters these birds must have constant privacy, otherwise they are likely to break the eggs or kill the chicks. A typical cockatoo clutch consists of one to four eggs, although the roseate species will lay five or six eggs. The incubation period last 25-32 days, and the youngsters vacate the nest about 10-14 weeks later. Offer the youngsters a varied diet, including fresh fruit.

Lories and lorikeets

The beautiful, brightly coloured lories and lorikeets are some of the most exquisite birds you can keep in captivity. Many lorikeets are no larger than a lovebird. Common lorikeets, such as the Swainson's, or rainbow, lorikeets, are considered pests in their native country but are relatively expensive to buy in the USA and Europe. Lorikeets are found in high mountainous areas right the way down to coastal areas, so they can adjust to quite a change in temperature, but do remember that they cannot cope with draughts. If you keep them in an outside aviary - and they will be happier outside than inside - they will tolerate a typical temperate winter, but it is a good idea to lock them in at night to protect them from cold draughts. If they are locked in a small inside enclosure, they will survive without heat. It is only the fairy lorikeet that needs heat during the winter.

Lorikeets spend most of their life off the ground in trees. It is probably better to describe them as climbers rather than fliers, because even though they can fly very well, they love to amuse themselves by jumping from one branch to another.

At one time, very few lorikeets were kept in the home, mainly because providing the right diet was difficult and very time-consuming; reproducing nectar is not easy! Lorikeets feed by crushing flowers and fruit in their beaks and sucking up the juice. They have a very weak ventriculus, or gizzard, which makes seed eating very difficult and potentially dangerous. Without a strong gizzard, the birds have no way of digesting seeds, so it is better to persevere

Right: *This brightly coloured, yellow-backed chattering lory is one of the larger species of lory that are commonly kept and bred in captivity. Its diet consists mainly of nectar and fruit. The larger lories are quite capable of destroying flimsy wooden aviaries.*

with nectar diets and not risk feeding seeds as an additive. Today, it is no longer necessary to prepare a homemade diet for lorikeets, as the commercial diets include every ingredient necessary for your bird, apart from a little fruit, which you must add yourself.

Before you buy lorikeets, remember that you will need plenty of time to look after them and also a certain amount of money, because even though feeding them has become easier, nectar is not cheap to buy. Furthermore, you must provide fresh nectar every day, as it soon deteriorates. (In fact, during warm weather you should change the nectar twice a day.) You cannot leave a supply of nectar for your lorikeets for a couple of days, as you would leave seed for a parrot.

Lorikeets are rather inept when it comes to mixing with other birds, so it is best to keep just a single pair of lories or lorikeets in an aviary with no other ground birds. Lorikeets are not recommended for planted aviaries, because even though they do not have strong

Right: The elegant Stella's lorikeet is a much sought after species. It has become more widely available in recent years following the success of captive breeding. Nevertheless, Stella's lories are delicate birds and are not recommended as a suitable species for the beginner to keep. The bird pictured here is a male.

Right: The beautiful rainbow lorikeets are some of the most strikingly coloured birds that you can find. This, and the fact that they are one of the more hardy species of lorikeets, makes them an ideal species for beginners.

Birds of the South Seas

Lories and lorikeets are found on various islands in Southeast Asia and the South Pacific, as well as in northern and eastern Australia. They are often found around coconut plantations in the South Seas. Lorikeets have longer tails than lories.

mandibles, they will chew and destroy almost any plants that you introduce. The main problem with keeping lorikeets is their droppings, which are extremely messy and do not necessarily fall to the bottom of the cage, as the birds tend to shoot them in all directions. Thorough cleaning every day is essential, otherwise the droppings will begin to build up and become a health hazard. If the birds are kept in an indoor aviary, it is a good idea to surround the lower third of the aviary with an easily cleanable material, such as glass or plastic, that you can wipe every day.

As with many species of birds, it is a good idea to let your lorikeets choose their own partners from half-a-dozen birds in one aviary. However, financial constraints may rule out this option and it is true that most single pairs do breed. Once you have a compatible pair, lorikeets are straightforward to breed. They usually breed at two to three years old and once they begin, they breed prolifically. These birds will happily accept a typical parrot nestbox, but make sure it is made of strong wood, because even though the birds' beaks are not particularly powerful, they do chew and are quite capable of destroying a thin nestbox within a few months. Drill several holes in the bottom to drain excess moisture from the birds' droppings. Even so, as the chicks grow you may occasionally need to remove the youngsters quickly and renew the bedding before putting the chicks back. Without this attention, the nestbox will start to smell very unpleasant. The usual clutch consists of two eggs, which take about 22-28 days to incubate. The young chicks fledge about 42-84 days after hatching, depending on the species.

Amazons

Amazons reach sizes of 24-53cm(9.5-21in) and will live between 30 and 70 years if kept in good health. These birds are commonly kept in captivity and can be housed acceptably in several different ways. Kept in an indoor cage, amazons make extremely amenable pets, for not only are they affectionate, but they are also talented talkers and produce considerably less noise than many of the larger parrots, such as cockatoos. However, if you do wish to keep an Amazon as a pet, start with a hand-reared youngster. Not only will the bird be tame, but you are also less likely to encounter health problems than with an imported bird. The most suitable species to keep as a caged pet is the blue-fronted or orange-winged Amazon. These have the correct temperament and are at the lower end of the price scale.

For breeding purposes, it is best to accommodate amazons in a large outdoor flight or aviary. Once acclimatized, they can withstand moderate winter conditions, but you will need to lock them in a protective shelter during severe weather conditions. It is becoming increasingly common for professional birdkeepers who breed amazons in large quantities to house them in suspended cages. These have the benefit of remaining clean and therefore hygienic and have proven to be very successful, but amateurs should begin with a standard parrot aviary.

Feeding amazons is very similar to macaws and cockatoos. They will thrive on a varied diet of large seeds and nuts, such as sunflower seeds, safflower seed, peanuts and pine

Right: The green-cheeked Amazon is mostly green, but has a striking red forehead and crown with some blue behind it. Males and females are similar and must be scientifically sexed. They are one of the more timid Amazon species and, although capable of making a noise, are quiet most of the time.

Below: The yellow-fronted Amazon has become more available in recent years. It has a pleasant nature, but is on the shy side. Watch out, however, because as with most species of Amazons their character can change dramatically in the breeding season, with painful results for you.

Below: The blue-fronted Amazon is the commonest Amazon kept in captivity and the cheapest to acquire. If you want a hand-reared parrot as a pet, then this is an excellent choice. They are easy to breed, but give them a good strong nestbox, as they have strong beaks.

New World parrots that travelled with Columbus

The 27 species of Amazons are native to northern Mexico, Central and South America, and the Caribbean islands of Trinidad and Tobago. They were first introduced into Europe by Columbus in 1492.

African grey parrot

A hand-reared African grey parrot makes a good pet, and is renowned for its powers of mimicry. Keep it in the same way as an Amazon parrot. These intelligent birds need plenty to keep them occupied. It is difficult to keep a grey parrot tame if you want to breed from it, as it will always prefer its partner to you.

nuts. Many people now feed their amazons a mixture of pulses. Fruit and vegetables are essential for good health. As with all parrots, Amazons need plenty of wood to chew, and so you will need to replace perches every couple of weeks.

The white-fronted Amazon is the only species that can be sexed by external means - the hen has green rather than red coverts (the 'shoulder flashes' of short feathers at the top front edges of the wings). The remaining species need scientific sexing. Amazons will breed successfully in anything from a small suspended cage to a large outdoor flight. As with the majority of parrots, it is rare for them to breed before they are three to four years old. Be sure to line the nestbox with an extra layer of wood to help protect it from the bird's destructive nature. Temperature and environment affect the number of clutches laid each season. For example, if kept in an outdoor environment, Amazons will only lay once a year, whereas birds kept indoors are more likely to lay twice in quick succession.

An average Amazon clutch consists of two to five white or creamy eggs, and the incubation period lasts 26-28 days. The chicks fledge 56-70 days later.

Touracos and tanagers

Touracos

Over the last few years, touracos have been increasingly kept in captivity. They vary in size from the white-cheeked touraco at 40cm(16in) up to the great blue touraco, which reaches a length of approximately 60cm(24in).

Touracos should be housed in a large aviary with ample room for exercise. They are very active birds and, although they are able to fly, they prefer to amuse themselves by jumping from perch to perch. Therefore, be sure to provide plenty of springy perches. During the colder winter months in temperate climates, touracos will need some type of heated quarters. Even when acclimatized, they are only relatively hardy, and once severe weather conditions set in, they should be locked in their heated back shelters.

Touracos are ideally housed with similarly sized ground birds, such as quails, partridges and pheasants. Out of the breeding season, you should experience few problems with this arrangement, but difficulties are likely to arise once the birds enter the breeding condition.

Touracos need a varied diet consisting mainly of chopped fruit, with supplements of mealworms, crickets, small amounts of mince and a good softbill mixture.

Part of the great appeal of keeping touracos is their strikingly friendly nature. This is especially true of hand-reared touracos, which without doubt must be among the most pleasurable birds

one can keep. However, there is a drawback and this is the cost of buying them in the first place. Even so, people still continue to collect and treasure these birds.

Sexing touracos is not an easy task, for not only do male and female birds look extremely similar, but as with parrots, two males or two females together often act as a 'pair'. Therefore, most, if not all, species of touracos will require scientific sexing.

Touracos have a preference for building their cup-shaped nests in dense bushes. However, to prevent the eggs falling through their flimsy and unsafe nests, it is a good idea to supply them with a basket. An average clutch consists of two white eggs, which hatch after about 20 days of incubation. The young will then fledge 28 days later. After their first breeding season, touracos will often breed twice a year, providing spring arrives early enough.

Relatives of the cuckoos

The touracos form a family of 19 species and are part of a larger grouping that includes the cuckoos and roadrunners. Touracos are native to Africa, where several species live in dense forest.

Below: The shining plumage and beautiful colours of the red-crested touraco, along with its active way of life, make this a gem of a softbill for any collection.

104

Tanagers

Although relatively small birds, at 12.5-18cm(5-7in), tanagers do live for about eight years, if maintained in good health. They are among the more delicate of birds and therefore need inside accommodation, ideally in a tropical house. It is quite acceptable, however, to keep tanagers outside during warm summer months, providing they have access to a shelter. If the temperature falls below 5°C(40°F), they will also need additional warmth.

Because tanagers are rather timid birds, they are much happier in a well-planted aviary, as this gives them a sense of security. In a tropical house, it is quite safe to mix tanagers with softbills of a similar size, although it is always advisable to check regularly that they are not being bullied. Tanagers love to bathe, and so be sure to provide a suitable water dish in their enclosure.

An ideal tanager diet consists of various diced fruits, accompanied by a good softbill mixture and some livefood, such as mealworms and crickets. They will also readily accept hummingbird nectar, although this can prove rather expensive. During the breeding season, livefoods such as buffalo worms, baby mealworms and baby crickets are essential.

Some species of tanagers can be sexed visually, the hens being distinguished by their duller appearance. Tanagers can be successful breeders in captivity, providing that you start with a healthy pair of birds. Keeping the breeding pair separate from other birds does help, as any disturbance may discourage their activities. Some will readily accept nestboxes; others prefer to nest in vegetation to lay their small clutch of two eggs. The incubation period lasts for approximately 13 days and fledging occurs 12-21 days later. In a tropical house situation, they are likely to produce two or three clutches each season. Never run out of livefood, even for a day, when there are young birds in the nestbox, as this will nearly always lead to the chicks being deserted.

Left: *The white-cheeked touraco is less expensive than other touracos to buy and the easiest to keep. As with all touracos, it is very active, but can also be messy with food and droppings.*

A large colourful family

Although most are based in the tropics and subtropics of the New World, these delightful birds are found at various times of the year over a wide area, from Canada through the USA to Central and South America. There are over 220 species in the family.

Right: *The blue-headed tanager is a good example of how impressive the plumage can be in many tanager species. This species is active nearly all the time and relatively easy to keep, as long as you keep it in a tropical house or in similar conditions where the birds can hide and feel safe in their captive environment.*

Bulbuls and thrushes

The 118 species of bulbuls range across Africa, India and southern Asia. They are common locally and make their presence known with their lively and inquisitive natures.

Bulbuls

Only a very small percentage of bulbul species are commonly kept in captivity. They vary in size from 18 to 23cm(7-9in) and have an average lifespan of up to eight years.

Bulbuls are best housed in a spacious, well-planted aviary. Because of their fine feathering, they have a low tolerance to cold climates, and this may cause problems during the acclimatization process. They are very sociable birds that will only live happily in groups within a large softbill aviary.

One of the plus points of keeping bulbuls is the simplicity of maintaining them in good health. The main drawback is their noticeable lack of bright and interesting coloration, although this is compensated for by their beautiful song. It is difficult to generalize on the temperament of bulbuls, for they all have very individual personalities. The best thing is to find someone who keeps bulbuls and seek advice on choosing the correct species for the environment you offer. Bulbuls need a varied diet with diced fruit, a good softbill mixture and a little livefood.

On entering the breeding season, bulbuls will need dense shrubs and bushes in which to construct their cup-shaped nests. Be sure to provide them with a variety of nest-building materials at this time. An average clutch consists of four eggs, which are incubated for a period of 13 days. The young chicks leave the nest 14-20 days later, depending on the species. Do remember, however, that bulbuls will not tolerate any human interference while they are breeding, and so leave them well alone during this time.

Above: The red-whiskered bulbul has unusual plumage and a pleasant nature, and so it is ideal for including in a large mixed aviary of softbills. It is normally easy to keep after the first week or so in a new environment.

Above: With its orange beak, the black bulbul stands out well in a planted green aviary. However, keep an eye on it, because as with all bulbuls, each one has a character of its own and occasionally you may get one that does not mix too well with other birds.

Pekin robin

The Pekin robin is an attractive thrushlike bird in the babbler family and widely kept in captivity. It is easy to keep in a well-planted aviary, but make sure that it has heated quarters for the winter in temperate climates. During the breeding season, the cock bird's song is melodious and is a definite way of distinguishing the sexes.

Left: The white-crested laughing thrush (a member of the babbler family) is widely kept in captivity. This is mainly because once they have settled in, they are relatively hardy and live for many years. Once you have obtained a confirmed pair of birds, they will breed easily, given a small nest basket and some privacy. They can be included in a mixed aviary if it is not crowded, but do not put them with smaller birds.

Familiar across the world

There are about 300 species in the true thrush family. They originated in the temperate and tropical regions of the Old World, but now occur almost worldwide. The allied babbler family has about 280 species.

Thrushes

Thrushes occupy a size range of 18-30cm(7-12in) and will live for ten years or more in healthy conditions. Housing them is relatively simple; all they require is a densely planted aviary with sufficient space for exercise. They thrive in an outside environment and will become hardy in temperate climates once acclimatized, more so than bulbuls. Thrushes love to bathe, as do most softbills, and you should indulge this passion by placing a larger, additional water dish in an easily accessible location within the aviary.

Many species are gregarious and will live happily within a mixed aviary. To avoid any possible disputes, it is best to house thrushes with birds of the same or of a slightly larger size. Laughing thrushes can be particularly vicious and aggressive, especially throughout the breeding season. Unfortunately, the aggressive behaviour of the laughing thrush has unfairly blackened the reputation of the majority of thrushes.

Be sure to obtain a good-quality softbill mixture for feeding your birds and also include supplements of soaked mynah pellets, diced fruit, various seeds, plus the all-important livefood, such as buffalo worms, mealworms and crickets.

Scientific sexing is the only means of accurately distinguishing between the sexes. Once the breeding season approaches, thrushes will need a varied selection of nestsites to choose from, the most popular being conifer trees. When they have settled on a breeding site, they will begin to construct their cup-shaped nests with the materials you have supplied. As soon as the eggs have been laid, it is essential to step up the amounts of livefood offered, as this will be the youngsters' staple diet. As with bulbuls, do not disturb them during this period.

A typical clutch consists of four or five eggs. Incubation lasts about 13 days and the young chicks fledge 12-21 days later.

Hummingbirds and sunbirds

Hummingbirds

Hummingbirds vary in size from the tiny bee hummingbird at 6.25cm(2.5in) to the giant species at up to 25cm(10in). They are not suitable birds for beginners to keep. They are complicated to maintain and you need to find out a great deal about a species before you attempt to keep it. Being so delicate, hummingbirds need to be kept in a tropical house and can only be permitted outside during exceptionally warm summer months.

Feeding is likely to present problems, as hummingbirds digest their food at an astounding rate. They consume more than their own weight in food each day and if they run out of food at any time, they are liable to become exhausted and die. Hummingbirds feed on nectar, which you can buy pre-made from pet stores to mix with water and dispense in special nectar feeders. You should always have more than one nectar dispenser available to your birds, just in case one leaks or is consumed exceptionally quickly. Supplement the nectar with live fruit flies. To remain healthy, encourage your birds to bathe by mist spraying them gently each day or by providing moistened foliage.

Hummingbirds are seldom mixed, especially with their own kind. Two males in the same aviary are likely to fight to the death, unless the aviary is large enough for the birds to keep out of each other's view. If you do attempt to mix hummingbirds, be sure to provide more than sufficient feeding points. The complications do not cease during the breeding season. In fact, they multiply, and this is why hummingbirds are rarely bred successfully in captivity.

Below: This splendid photograph of a blue-chinned sapphire hummingbird demonstrates the complete mastery of flying and hovering that these birds have evolved. Hummingbirds can be difficult to keep, but once you have an acclimatized bird, you will always be amazed at their flying skills, no matter how often you see them. Hummingbirds are not very often bred in captivity, but the success rate is increasing.

Hovering birds from the tropics of the New World

Most of the 319 species of hummingbirds live in the tropical zones of Central and South America, but a few species range north into Canada and south into Patagonia.

108

Sunbirds

Physically distinguishable by their slightly larger size, sunbirds require much the same care as hummingbirds. They are best housed in a tropical house or within an indoor environment that has access to an outdoor flight. Although a little hardier than hummingbirds, sunbirds cannot cope with even the mildest winter conditions found in temperate climates and should be allowed outdoors only during the warmest summer months. If housed in a large, well-planted tropical house, it is quite possible to mix sunbirds with suitable birds of a similar size, such as tanagers. Although sunbirds are easier to maintain than hummingbirds, they are also unsuitable for beginners.

Unlike hummingbirds, sunbirds do not hover when feeding and so it is important to ensure that their food is easily accessible from the ground or a perch. Supplement their basic diet of nectar with fruit flies and diced sweet fruits. Some species may need colour food to keep their plumage in outstanding condition.

Sunbirds can be easily sexed visually, the duller appearance and olive-grey plumage distinguishing the hen from the cock. Although the breeding success rate for sunbirds is considerably higher than that for hummingbirds, they are still extremely difficult to breed in captivity. Success is most likely if pairs are housed separately throughout the breeding season. The eggs are incubated for 14 days and the young should fledge a further 14 days later.

Old World reflections of the hummingbirds

Although not related to hummingbirds, sunbirds mirror their small size and dazzling colours. More than half of the 104 species of sunbirds live in tropical Africa; others are found across southern Asia and into the Pacific islands.

Above: The spectacular plumage of the male scarlet-chested sunbird explains why so many birdkeepers admire it. This very active bird can be housed with hummingbirds in a good-sized tropical house and, once settled, will live for many years. Treat it carefully to begin with, as it may suffer from stress. The female is very drab in comparison and breeding the birds is difficult.

White-eyes and flycatchers

White-eyes

Although relatively small birds, with a size range of 10-17cm (4-6.7in), white-eyes do live up to ten years if well maintained. Since they are particularly delicate birds that cannot withstand cold weather, the most suitable housing arrangement is a large, well-planted indoor flight. They must be kept in a heated environment. It is quite acceptable, however, to place them in an outdoor aviary during the warmer summer months. Not only are white-eyes bright and alert, but they are also exceedingly sociable. For this reason, do not house them alone. They will live very happily in groups and are highly compatible with similarly sized species, such as waxbills.

White-eyes will flourish on a diet of diced fruit, fine softbill food and good-quality nectar solution. They will also relish a small amount of livefood, which you should increase for breeding purposes. Compared to other small nectivores, such as hummingbirds and sunbirds, white-eyes are easy to maintain and this accounts for their ever-increasing popularity. As for most small birds, daily bathing is essential and you can achieve this by providing a shallow dish of fresh clean water each day.

White-eyes cannot be sexed by their appearance. Although performed on a regular basis in captivity, breeding white-eyes can prove to be rather difficult. It is essential to provide the breeding pair with ample nesting material within a peaceful environment. If mating is successful, the clutch will consist of two to four blue-green eggs. These hatch after 12 days of incubation by both parents and the young chicks fledge about 14 days later.

Bright birds from the warmth of the Old World

The 85 species of white-eyes, or zosterops, as they are also known, live in India, Africa, Southeast Asia, Australasia and western China. The common name reflects the circle of white feathers around the eye.

Above: The Cape white-eye is shy by nature and sometimes lost in a densely planted aviary, but this is what it likes. As with all white-eyes, these birds love livefood and many people keep them in their tropical houses as an effective control against small insects, such as aphids, that attack the plants.

Left: The white-eyes are shy birds, but always active. They fit in well with almost all other softbills and so you find them included in most mixed collections. Keep them relatively sheltered in the summer, but in winter they are best housed inside.

Below: The Indian blue-throated flycatcher can be kept without problems in a mixed collection or in a relatively small inside enclosure. Always have plenty of livefood available to keep these birds in peak condition and to maintain their astounding blue colour. If fed correctly, the bird's plumage will shine, as here.

Two separate families that span the world

There are two families of flycatchers: the tyrant flycatchers in the New World that range from Canada to Patagonia, and the quite separate Old World flycatchers found across Africa, Eurasia and into Australia. The ones kept in captivity are members of the Old World family.

Flycatchers

These birds can vary greatly in size, from 12.5cm(5in) for the spotted flycatcher up to the Asian paradise flycatcher, in which the cock birds measure at least 50cm(20in), including their long tail feathers. Flycatchers are best housed in a large outdoor aviary during the summer months, but when the weather starts to get cold they are happier brought in, and be sure to provide a snug night-time shelter with the facility for artificial light. Acclimatizing these birds can have its complications; it is vital not to rush things and to avoid taking any risks. If you are a beginner, flycatchers are not suitable birds for you to start with. Wait until you have gained some experience within the hobby before keeping these birds.

Flycatchers feed mainly on a variety of livefoods, such as mealworms, buffalo worms, crickets and fruit flies. A good-quality softbill food and various softbill pellets are also essential. Tropical species also need a little nectar and a good pre-made softbill food.

To maintain these birds in excellent appearance and health, it is essential for them to bathe daily. Provide a shallow bathing dish and you could also try spraying them with a fine mist sprayer.

Sexing flycatchers depends on the species. With the African paradise flycatcher, for example, the hen has shorter tail feathers. Once in breeding condition, flycatchers build their cup-shaped nests in dense shrubs or bushes, although some species prefer to use a nestbox, either a half open-fronted one or one with a hole drilled in it to match the size of the birds concerned. Incubation and rearing duties are shared equally between the cock and hen. Incubation lasts 16 days and the young fledge 14 days later. If they are housed in a large aviary, the young will not have any problems when they fledge; in a small enclosure, it is best to remove them just in case the parents want to breed again.

Mynahs and starlings

Lively birds from the forests of the Old World

Mynahs and starlings belong to the same family of birds and were originally confined to the warm forests of the Old World. Because of distribution by man, starlings of various species are now found throughout the world, except in South America. In captivity, their average lifespan can vary from eight to twenty-five years, depending on the species.

Mynahs

Mynah birds are commonly kept as caged pets and this is perfectly acceptable, providing that you obtain a suitable cage. Their size, 20-45cm(8-18in), demands a spacious enclosure and specially designed mynah bird cages are available from pet stores. It is also possible to keep mynah birds outdoors; they can be acclimatized relatively easily, although they need to be locked into a snug and heated shelter once the winter approaches. Damp, foggy weather is a particular hazard and can easily kill them. It is possible to keep mynahs within a mixed collection, providing the accompanying birds are the same size or larger; any smaller species run the risk of being eaten.

Mynah birds' immense popularity is largely due to their astounding talents as mimics. The most commonly kept species is the greater hill mynah, whose cheeky and boisterous personality only adds to its appeal. However, mynahs do have the disadvantage of being extremely messy. This is why it is best to house them in the specially designed mynah cages, which have high sides to keep their copious droppings within the enclosure.

Their omnivorous diet should consist of various diced fruit, a good-quality softbill food, supplemented with mynah pellets and a few mealworms. It is essential for mynahs to bathe regularly, particularly so if they are housed indoors. Because they are so messy, it is essential to observe scrupulous hygiene in their enclosures. They are susceptible to foot infections, although these can be avoided by scrubbing or replacing the perches regularly.

The only accurate method of distinguishing the sexes is by scientific sexing. Mynah birds are being successfully bred in captivity much more than in the past, although it is still not an easy task. To encourage breeding, provide your birds with a nestbox and various nesting materials. If successful, the clutch should consist of two or three blue eggs with brown specks. After 14 days, the chicks should hatch and it is at this point that a constant supply of livefood is essential. When the chicks vacate the nest, 20 days later, check that the parents are not attempting to breed again, as this could lead to them fatally attacking their young. If you have kept a mynah for many years as a pet and you decide you want to breed from it, remember it will probably not remain tame.

Left: *The greater hill mynah is a real character and best known for its ability to mimic sounds and voices. This is the most common species of mynah kept in captivity and until recently was only kept for its talents. In the past few years they have been bred in many collections. For such success, they must be given plenty of privacy.*

Starlings

Their size range of 18-56cm(7-22in) and tough personality demand that starlings require a spacious outdoor environment. Starlings have been known to live contentedly in groups, even though they have aggressive tendencies. If you are a beginner or have any doubts, however, it is best to keep them in pairs.

Starlings' feeding requirements are very similar to those of mynah birds, this being various diced fruit, a good-quality softbill mix, mynah pellets and a little livefood. You may find that starlings accept a larger amount of livefood than mynahs. Starlings do love to bathe and it is vital not to discourage them, as it is an essential part of their normal healthy regime.

Some species of starlings can be sexed by visual means, although for total accuracy it is advisable to have them sexed

scientifically. Breeding starlings is fairly easy if you start with a true pair. Provide them with a suitably sized nestbox lined with wood chippings or twigs. A typical starling clutch consists of two or three green-blue eggs with red or dark blue specks. The chicks hatch after 16 days incubation and leave the nest 21 days later. Remember to remove the chicks at the earliest opportunity after they have fledged.

Below: Purple glossy starlings have amazing plumage that is seen to best advantage if you can keep the birds in an aviary that gets plenty of sunlight to show off the different colours. The best way to keep the birds is in a colony of a few pairs.

Above: With its orange breast, the delightful spreo starling has pride of place in many collections, especially in mixed collections of softbills. You can keep these birds in a colony and, indeed, they look very good flying around together in a large aviary. Make sure you provide the birds with sufficient extra nestboxes so that they have plenty of choice; this will prevent them fighting.

Waxwings and barbets

Waxwings

Most waxwings measure about 18cm(7in) long and such a size presents no housing complications. Being particularly hardy birds, they can be kept outdoors all year round without additional heat. However, they do need a shelter to provide cover from wind and rain. You can safely house these highly gregarious birds within a mixed collection of similarly sized birds and yet experience very little, if any, incompatibility problems. In fact, they are so simple to maintain that they are an ideal choice for beginners interested in starting up a mixed collection of softbills.

Feeding waxwings presents no problems, as they will thrive on a standard good-quality softbill food, and will also take diced fruit, insects and a limited amount of seed and greenfood.

Distinguishing between the sexes in waxwings is only possible by scientific means. In practice, however, many people do not bother to do so; they just assume that there must be a pair within their collection of birds. This explains why waxwings are not bred on a regular basis.

During the breeding season, waxwings will nest at various sites within the aviary - usually in vegetation - and, as with most birds, once they start to nest the best thing to do is to leave them alone. A typical clutch consists of two or three eggs, the incubation period lasts for approximately 14 days and the young chicks fledge 21 days later.

Right: The strikingly marked D'Arnaud's barbet, an African species, must have more insects in its diet to remain healthy in captivity.

Adaptable travellers

Waxwings are distributed over a vast area of northern Europe, Asia and North America, with migratory tendencies during the winter months to the southern areas of their respective ranges.

Left: The pretty Japanese waxwing is easy to keep and an excellent bird for the beginner. They are kept on a very large scale and the price is normally fairly affordable. This species is hardy and seems able to cope with most conditions.

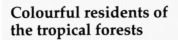

Colourful residents of the tropical forests

Barbets are at home in the tropical forests of the world, with more than half of the known species found in Africa. These conspicuous birds are also found in southern Asia and in Central and South America.

Barbets

The various striking species of barbets can vary in the size range 15-25cm(6-10in). They can be housed in a densely planted aviary, although heated quarters are vital throughout the winter, for even when acclimatized, barbets are not hardy birds. They are extremely active birds and are amusing to watch in the aviary. However, the drawback of such self-assured behaviour is that they can become aggressive, not only towards other species, but in some cases also towards humans. For this reason, do not mix them with other birds.

The general care for barbets involves providing ample material, such as logs, on which they can exercise their tremendously strong beaks. It is also important to provide a suitably shallow bathing dish so that the birds remain healthy and in good condition.

The typical daily consumption of food for barbets should include good-quality softbill food, mynah pellets, diced fruit and insects. The

amounts of fruit and insects will differ with the species; the New World species, for example, tend to rely more on fruit, whereas the African species of barbets are primarily insect eaters.

In the majority of barbet species it is not possible to confirm whether they are male or female purely on their appearance. As the breeding season approaches, it is advisable to monitor the behaviour of the cock bird closely, as it has been known for them to turn particularly brutal towards their mates. When the breeding season starts, provide your birds with either a suitably sized nestbox or a hollow log in which they can nest. A typical clutch consists of up to three eggs, the incubation period lasts 14 days and the youngsters vacate the nest 21 days later.

Left: Fire-tufted barbets are best kept in pairs. Do not mix them with other birds, as they are aggressive. Be careful when catching them; they have a strong bite and will not hesitate to use it.

Rollers and kingfishers

Rollers

The comparatively large size of rollers, in the range 30-40cm (12-16in), demands a high-roofed and spacious outdoor flight. Although relatively hardy once acclimatized, they will also require a snug shelter in which to keep warm during particularly severe conditions. Rollers are really only compatible with ground birds; do not attempt to mix them with smaller birds, as they are liable to turn aggressive both in and out of the breeding season.

Rollers are primarily insectivorous in their eating habits and this can prove rather expensive. They will accept the majority of insects, although locusts and crickets often prove to be their favourites. They will also readily take minced ox-heart.

There are no external differences between male and female rollers, and so scientific sexing is the only way of telling them apart. Although the successful breeding of rollers has increased considerably over the last few years, such success has only a very low chance of becoming consistent. Rollers need a horizontal rather than a vertical nestbox in which to lay their clutch of up to five eggs. These are incubated for 18 days and the young chicks fledge approximately 28 days later. It is advisable to remove the nestbox at this time to prevent the parents attempting to breed again. You can almost guarantee that the parents will attack the young within a few weeks of fledging, so remove them from the aviary as soon as possible to protect them.

Above: Racquet-tailed rollers are attractive birds, especially in flight. They are shy when you first introduce them into the aviary, but soon become tame once they have settled in, especially if you offer them livefood. They are not the hardiest of rollers, so lock them in when the weather is bad.

Dazzling acrobats from Africa to Australia

Most species of rollers live in Africa, south of the Sahara, but some are found across the Middle East and through southern China to Australia and the Solomons. The common name describes their rolling acrobatic flight patterns.

116

Kingfishers

Smaller than rollers, kingfishers can vary in the size range 20-28cm (8-11in). With the exception of the considerably smaller species, such as the pygmy kingfisher, which can be kept inside, it is best to house kingfishers outdoors in a large well-planted aviary. Once they are acclimatized, kingfishers become only fairly hardy and will therefore need locking in throughout any bad weather conditions.

A plus point in keeping kingfishers must be their magnificent plumage. However, problems can arise from their tendency to turn aggressive towards other species. This compatibility difficulty can be helped by housing the birds within an aviary that is large enough for the birds to keep out of each other's way. In such an aviary, you should be able to mix kingfishers with a wide variety of species with little problem.

Just like rollers, kingfishers are primarily insectivorous and, contrary to popular belief, many species will not eat fish. Suitable livefoods include mealworms, buffalo worms, crickets and locusts. The fish-eating species will readily accept sand eels, - available from pet stores.

The majority of kingfisher species have no external sexual differences. Complications are likely to arise with breeding kingfishers because they are hole-breeders and will not accept traditional nestboxes. Providing a specially constructed wall that the birds can burrow into is one way of fulfilling their needs. Alternatively, they are likely to accept a large, tightly compacted bale of peat with a hole about 30cm(12in) across cut out of the plastic so that the birds can gain access to dig out a nest. If breeding is successful, the 2-3 eggs are incubated by both parents for 18 days and the young chicks fledge about 28 days later.

Above: The white-breasted kingfisher has delightful plumage, but an aggressive nature, so do not mix it with smaller birds. It is difficult to breed in captivity without plenty of patience.

Vibrant and cosmopolitan

Kingfishers are found in almost every region of the world, but they are most numerous and diverse in Southeast Asia and across into Australia.

Below: The kookaburra is a relative of the kingfisher, but much easier to keep and breed in captivity. It is not an active bird but does have a great personality. Its most distinctive feature is its amazing call, which is very loud indeed, but only used once or twice a day. The kookaburra may prove unpopular with neighbours, as its call is often heard early in the morning!

Jays and magpies

Jays

Jays grow to about 30-35cm(12-14in) and are quite happy in a large outdoor aviary or flight. With the exception of the very exotic species, the majority of jays become considerably hardy once acclimatized and so can be kept outside all year round. It is essential, however, to provide a snug shelter for them, even though they do not need locking in every night.

The great simplicity of maintaining jays in excellent health and their striking appearance account for their appeal. And their active and inquisitive nature provides amusement for hours. However, they do have an aggressive side to their nature and this strictly limits their companions within the aviary. Ground birds, such as pheasants and partridges, are quite suitable, but any smaller flying birds run the risk of being attacked or even eaten. Feed your jays a mixture of various diced fruits, a good-quality softbill food, mynah pellets and small amounts of livefood and mince.

There are no external differences between the cock and hen birds, so you must rely on scientific sexing to guarantee that you have a pair. At the beginning of the breeding season, jays will start to construct their cup-shaped nests in any nearby shrubbery, and it is often a good idea to provide them with a platform or basket, as their nests are usually too flimsy to survive the season. Once a bonded pair have become established, they will make frequent attempts to lay. In fact, it is quite common for jays to breed successfully in captivity. An average clutch consists of four eggs, incubation lasts for 16 days and fledging occurs 21 days later.

Striking members of the widespread crow family

Jays and magpies belong to one of the two subfamilies of the crow family, which has just over 100 species and reaches across the world. The jays are particularly colourful in the New World, while the magpies are most diverse in the Southeast Asian part of their equally wide range.

Right: Azure jays have interesting plumage and can be recommended to anyone. Like all jays, they require plenty of livefood to keep them in good health and to encourage breeding. They can be kept with ground birds, but will need some privacy if you want to breed them. Often, a long, narrow aviary with a nest area at the back will help to make them feel more secure. If the aviary is large enough, you do not need to remove the young straight after fledging; indeed, two broods can occupy an aviary with their parents, but keep an eye on them in case of problems.

Magpies

Most magpies are considerably larger than jays, measuring 33-66cm (13-26in). Hardy once acclimatized, these birds will thrive in a large and spacious aviary. They are extremely lively birds, and are also liable to become highly aggressive. As with jays, this restricts the species that can be safely housed with them. The only really suitable companions are ground birds. Even so, they should be the larger species, since small partridges and quail would be attacked.

With the exception of their compatibility conflicts, magpies are very easy to maintain in captivity. And being scavengers, they will readily accept a range of foods. The same diet as that for jays is quite acceptable, including mynah pellets, various diced fruits, and small amounts of livefood and mince.

It is always best to have magpies scientifically sexed, rather than rely on the minor differences between them. Magpies are commonly bred in captivity. Successful breeding can be encouraged either by providing the pair with an old magpie nest from the wild or by placing a platform or basket high up in a dense tree, such as a conifer. The higher this platform is placed, the more secure the birds will feel. Disturb the birds as little as possible throughout the breeding season and provide ample amounts of livefood. Three to six eggs form a typical clutch, the incubation period lasts for 17 days and fledging occurs approximately 21 days later. To avoid attacks from the parents, remove the chicks from the nest as soon as they are fledged and have begun to feed themselves.

Above: The majestic red-billed blue magpie is an easy bird to keep, being very hardy once acclimatized and, like all magpies, easy to feed. If possible, house them in a reasonably large aviary, *as this helps to give them privacy and prevents their long and beautiful tails from becoming unkempt. Once you have obtained a compatible pair, they breed easily and will do so every year.*

Toucans and hornbills

Toucans and hornbills are probably the least commonly kept birds by the private birdkeeper. They are magnificently colossal birds that require huge enclosures with large heated shelters and this, in conjunction with the great expense of buying them, is the reason why they are more commonly seen in zoos and bird parks.

Toucans

These substantial birds require housing within an extensive outside flight with access to a heated shelter. Even when acclimatized, toucans remain rather sensitive to temperatures below freezing point. They need to be locked in every night. Since toucans are rather antisocial, it is not advisable to mix them. Although it is possible to house them with the larger species of ground birds, to be on the safe side, it is best to keep pairs individually.

Toucans feed mainly on various diced fruits, some livefood and soaked mynah pellets, but for an occasional treat they may be offered whole mice or pinkies (newborn mice).

Although hens can sometimes be distinguished by their smaller beaks, this is far from a reliable method of sexing toucans. Scientific sexing is the only sure way. The breeding success rate of toucans in captivity has increased in recent years, but is still relatively uncommon. Success can be encouraged by providing a hollow log as the favoured breeding site. Alternatively, a nestbox positioned at an angle of 45° with a long tunnel leading to a nesting site may encourage breeding. Two or three white eggs form a typical clutch, the incubation period lasts approximately 19 days and the young chicks vacate the nest about 50 days later. Toucans are far from model parents and any disturbance will only make them worse. If they abandon their chicks, it is possible to hand rear the youngsters, although this is not common practice.

Right: The impressive toco toucan is the ultimate bird for any serious collection. With its beautiful plumage and magnificent bill, not many birds can match it. It can be bred in captivity, but this bird is really for experts and those who can afford to buy it and cope with the high cost of its food.

Tropical fruit pickers

Toucans live wild in the tropical forests of Central and South America, using their large but light beaks to pick fruit from nearby branches. There are about 40 species in the family.

Right: Compared with its very large relatives, which are best left in zoos, the red-billed hornbill is quite easy to keep in captivity. With a spacious enclosure and plenty of privacy, it regularly breeds in captivity. However, this species is not recommended for a novice birdkeeper, as it is expensive to keep, requiring plenty of fruit and livefood.

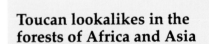

Toucan lookalikes in the forests of Africa and Asia

Although not as colourful, the hornbills bear a reasonable resemblance to their American counterparts, to which they are not related. There are about 40 species in the hornbill family.

Hornbills

Hornbills vary in size from the red-billed at 45cm(18in) up to the
great Indian and rhinoceros hornbills, which reach up to 90cm(36in)
in length. These birds need a huge and sturdy, well-planted aviary
with many strong perches to hold their colossal weight. Although
hardier than toucans, hornbills will still need locking in each night
throughout severe winter conditions. The shelter should provide a
temperature of at least 3-4°C(37-39°F), as they are particularly
susceptible to frostbite. Hornbills should only be housed in
individual pairs for both breeding and safety purposes. Even the
larger species of ground birds are likely to be attacked.

   Hornbills daily consume vast amounts of diced fruit,
chopped meat, insects (such as locusts) and soaked mynah
pellets. The food these birds consume does demand a rather
expensive budget, so be prepared.

   Scientific sexing is the best way to determine the sex of a
bird. On entering the breeding season, in addition to
providing a suitably sized and positioned nestbox, you
will also need to provide the cock bird with plenty of
mud and damp clay. He uses this to seal the hen bird
into the nestbox, leaving a small hole through which
he passes food to her. The hen then lays a clutch of up
to four eggs, incubates them for 28-40 days and when
the chicks are ready to fledge, approximately 28-56
days later, she will break through the mud barrier.

   Not surprisingly, toucans and hornbills are not
commonly kept in captivity and such an
undertaking can only be recommended to
birdkeepers with extensive experience.

Index to birds

Page numbers in **bold** indicate major text references and panels. Page numbers in *italics* indicate captions and annotations. Other text entries are shown in normal type.

Picture credits

Principal photographer
The majority of the photographs featured in this book have been taken by and are © Cyril Laubscher.

Commissioned photography
Neil Sutherland © Colour Library Books. These are indicated by page number and position of the photograph on the page, i.e. (B)Bottom, (T)Top, (C)Centre, (BL)Bottom left, etc: 12(BL), 12-13(B), 13(T), 14, 15(T), 16(T), 17, 19(B), 22-3, 24-5, 28(TR), 29, 38(R), 39, 40(BR), 41, 44(TR), 44-5(BC), 45(BR).

Additional photographs: Ideas into Print: 18-19(T), 30(T), 38(TL), 43(TR).

Artists
The artwork illustrations on pages 25(TR), and 31(T) of the book have been prepared by Rod Ferring, © Colour Library Books.

Author's acknowledgment
The author would like to thank Suki Butt for the many hours that she spent turning the original tape recordings and messy notes into the first readable draft of the manuscript.

Publishers' acknowledgments
The publishers would like to thank the following people for making their birds and aviaries available for photography: Ghalib-Al-Nasser and Janice Foxton, George Anderdon, Paul and June Bailey, Don and Irene Bardgett, Fred Barnicoat, Bob Beeson, Harry Bishop, Trevor Bonneywell, Allan Brooker, Trevor and Maura Buckell, Irene Christie, Terry and Jean Cole, Dulcie and Freddie Cooke, Marion Cripps, Alain and Janine Delille, Bill Dobbs and Jean Kozicka, Phil Dobinson, Alan Donnelly, Bruce Duthie, Ken and Shirley Epps, Keith and Margaret Ferry, Ray Fisk, Ken Furssedon, Alan Gibson, Rodney and Joan Hamilton, Fred Hill and Dinah Walker, Roger Green, John Harris, Geoff and Sandra Hornsby, Colin and Lesley Jackson, Ron James, Tim Kemp, Deborah Kenyon, Michel Klat, Errol Laubscher, Shirley and George Lawton, Gary McCarthy, Stanley Maughan, Albert Newsham, Judith Nicholas, Doug Nudd, Arthur and Gwen O'Bray, Mike and Denise O'Neill, Ron Oxley, Andy and Audrey Perkins, Les Perry, Brian Pettitt, Mick and Beryl Plose, Janet Ralph, Fred and Ken Rix, Walter and Jenny Savoury, Raymond Sawyer, Stan Sindel, George Smith, Jane Smith, Jack Stunnell, Nigel Taboney, Peter Thumwood, Joyce Venner.

Aviary models on pages 38-41 constructed by Daniel Rogers.